The LIRT Library
Instruction Handbook

THE LIRT LIBRARY INSTRUCTION HANDBOOK

Edited by

MAY BROTTMAN
Media Specialist
Glenbrook North High School
Northbrook, Illinois

and

MARY LOE
Coordinator of Library Instruction
State University College of New York
Oswego, New York

A product of the 1985
"World Book – American Library Association Goals Award"
to Library Instruction Round Table (LIRT)
of American Library Association

1990
LIBRARIES UNLIMITED, INC.
Englewood, Colorado

LIBRARIES UNLIMITED, INC.
P.O. Box 3988
Englewood, CO 80155-3988

Library of Congress Cataloging-in-Publication Data

The LIRT library instruction handbook / edited by May Brottman and Mary Loe as a product of the 1985 World Book-American Library Association Goals Award to Library Instruction Round Table (LIRT) of American Library Association.
    xi, 125 p. 22x28 cm.
    Includes bibliographical references.
    ISBN 0-87287-664-0
    1. Library orientation--Handbooks, manuals, etc. I. Brottman, May, 1930- . II. Loe, Mary, 1944- . III. Library Instruction Round Table (American Library Association)
Z711.2.L77   1990
025.5'6--dc20
                                    90-5509
                                      CIP

Contents

PART VI
BIBLIOGRAPHY

Preface

This handbook, the product of an American Library Association and World Book Goals Award Grant with additional funding by the Library Instruction Round Table (LIRT), has been written, critiqued, and rewritten by members of the ALA Library Instruction Round Table. The purpose of this handbook is to provide practical, step-by-step advice to enable institutions to develop programs based on sound theory and to enable practicing instruction librarians to evaluate and improve their own programs. In addition, it is designed to promote an element of standardization in developing programs in different types of libraries so that the next important step can be undertaken—that of developing an articulated curriculum for teaching access skills and information handling that will begin in children's early life and progress through each level of their education and beyond. With the creation of successful programs based on similar rationale and according to a specified sequence of tested strategies, the probability of achieving an information-literate population is greatly enhanced.

The LIRT Committee envisioned an audience for this handbook reaching beyond the immediate circle of practicing librarians. As a guide to library instruction programs and research across the spectrum of libraries, it can help prepare library and information science students for their future role as educators in any information arena they may choose. In a climate of growing concern for teaching critical thinking and problem solving skills, this handbook highlights related information access and processing skills inherent in thoughtful library use at all educational levels. With administrative interest and collegial teamwork, library instruction programs can play a central role in this educational goal. And in the broader environment of business and professional organizations, the pace of new, computerized, information formats is feeding the need for quicker, more efficient access to research. Special libraries and information specialists are adjusting to meet these changing needs.

The handbook was prepared by experienced bibliographic instruction librarians and supplemented by an editorial board of more than forty LIRT members representing libraries of all types: school; academic, including community college; public; and special; large and small; urban and rural. We based its content on a thorough literature review and a nationwide survey of public, school, academic, and special librarians. The literature review determined what had already been written about library instruction; the survey provided the authors with information about what library practitioners felt they already had and what they needed to learn.

An initial draft was completed by the various authors. The draft handbook was then used and reviewed at a two-day LIRT ALA preconference workshop by thirty-five practicing bibliographic librarians from all types of libraries. Their comments and evaluations were submitted to the major authors for incorporation into this revised handbook.

The introductory essay by Evan Farber covers the state of the art in bibliographic instruction programs. This is followed by a second essay that covers the important role of instruction in information access skills and the integration of resources other than textbooks as an integral part of the curriculum at all levels of education. Knowledge acquired in this active manner serves as a base for additional experiences that nourish both problem solving and critical thinking skills through the evaluation of sundry sources of information. The need for standardization in the organization of library instruction programs is delineated. The general overview chapter presents the steps taken in the process of developing an instruction program common to all types of libraries, such as assessing needs, selecting and analyzing a program's audience, and practical considerations to be taken into account when developing a program.

The remaining chapters are each devoted to a specific type of library—academic and junior college, public, school, and special—and similarly organized in terms of content. Each begins with an overview of the need for instruction programs in that type of institution and develops strategies for planning, conducting a needs assessment, developing goals, and obtaining administration and staff support. The steps for developing a specific instruction program are then examined in detail: analyzing the program's audience, identifying and stating the program's purpose, setting objectives, selecting teaching methods, and developing curriculum. The practical considerations of each type of program are examined in terms of managing and staffing the program; anticipating the additional costs of establishing and running a program; promoting the program;

scheduling instruction activities; starting up, and evaluation. Each section includes selected examples of bulletins, evaluation forms, publicity, and a bibliography of classic and current works. The final detailed bibliography focuses on works published in the 1980s and is organized by type of library and subject.

Many individuals have been important to the successful completion of this handbook project. The World Book—ALA Goals Award won in 1985 by the Library Instruction Round Table of the American Library Association made the project possible. A complete list of all involved and their role in the project is appended to this volume.

A crucial member of this entire project has been Georgeanne Moore. In addition to being the administrative assistant for the project, she prodded the director, May Brottman, whenever she strayed. At all of the meetings, it was Georgeanne who made sure that everyone had a copy of the right drafts at the right time. She has retyped this handbook many times and was also responsible for mailing the 2,600 surveys and recording the status of all the returns. Without her willing and capable help, it would have been difficult to complete the project. Our thanks also to Nina Tsuneta, who typed the final manuscript with care, and to SUNY/UUP for a grant that helped with the final editing tasks.

May Brottman
Mary Loe

Acknowledgments

When the handbook was completed in May 1986, the following appeared in the introduction.

No director of any project either in business or in the public sector has had the good fortune to work with a group as willing, dedicated, and committed to their field and to the idea of instruction in the use of libraries as the group I was fortunate to work with. I admit to having set some pretty grim deadlines, but each and every person met them all. I became aware of the uniqueness of this group at the American Library Association midwinter conference in January 1986. Everyone had a responsibility for an all day meeting on Friday, January 17. The day arrived and so did forty people. I was touched and excited—for every single person had done what they were supposed to do. Every first draft was ready and everyone had a copy of everything that was done. From that day on with every deadline, the same thing occurred. So, if this project succeeds [and it did], it is because of the dedication and hard work of each one of the people mentioned [in the appendix]. And to them I say with much humility—it was a privilege to work with them. There are no words sufficient to express my admiration and thanks for the support and dedication of each and everyone who contributed to this project. May Brottman, Director. LIRT World Book—ALA Goals Award Project May 1986

PART I
PLANNING AND MANAGING LIBRARY INSTRUCTION
The Common Ground

Reflections on Library Instruction

Evan Ira Farber

Library Director
Earlham College
Richmond, Indiana

The idea of librarians teaching their users how to better use their libraries is hardly a new one. Terms such as library instruction, information skills teaching, reader instruction, user orientation, bibliographic instruction, and others can be found in the literature well back into the nineteenth century. Today the most frequently found terms are bibliographic instruction and library instruction—the former used primarily by most college and university librarians and the latter by school and public librarians as well as by some in higher education. The methods and structures of individual programs range widely; there are almost an infinite number of variations, since the individual method and structure will probably be tailored to fit the needs of a specific library and clientele. There is, however, a single purpose, a basic thrust, to all the efforts. That basic thrust is, of course, to help the various clienteles use their libraries' resources more effectively.

Though the idea of user instruction may be an old one, it is only over the past few decades that it has assumed the proportions of a major professional movement. It now has several important organizations devoted to it within the profession and, indeed, the Bibliographic Instruction Section is now the largest of The Association of College & Research Libraries' fourteen sections. There are full-time positions in several types of libraries that are specifically devoted to user instruction and many more that include it as part of their responsibilities. As a result, at least a few library schools offer courses on user instruction and many more acknowledge its significance by including it as part of other courses, usually reference. Finally, a sizable number of books and hundreds of articles on the subject have been published, and at least one professional periodical is devoted to it.

Why this recent surge of interest in teaching library use? After all, libraries have been around a long time. There are two factors. The first is that phenomenon, now almost a cliché, known as the information explosion. A cliché it might be, but the incredible increase in the amount of information available over the past few decades *has* been phenomenal, and anyone seeking information on almost any topic is immediately faced with more sources than one can use, more certainly than one can digest. Nor is it just the number of sources that's confusing, but also the variety of sources, often with conflicting data and conclusions. The second factor is the increase in the number and in the complexity of library tools—catalogs, indexes, abstracting services, handbooks, subject bibliographies—that should be used to access and sort through the enormous amount of available information. Anyone with even the most basic knowledge of libraries can find *something* on almost any subject. It is, however, becoming increasingly difficult to find the most useful and most reliable information unless one knows the appropriate tools that can help one find the information and sort one's way through it.

Permitting users to find reliable information more easily then, is the immediate rationale for teaching library use. There may well be, however, an even more important, long-range reason. We want our clientele to be more effective in whatever they do, as professionals, as business people, as citizens, as parents. Increasingly, being effective means having access to appropriate information and then, on the basis of that information, acting. In many ways, our society is rapidly becoming—if, indeed, it's not already become—an information-based one, and in such a society success or failure will increasingly be measured in terms of one's ability to find, organize, and use information. We want our students to do better work, to become more independent learners. We want our adults to become more intelligent, more discriminating consumers of information. We want all members of our different clienteles to become full participants in our information-based society. Learning how to use a library effectively may not guarantee that, but it can surely help, and it may well provide the impulse which will help attain that participation in other ways.

But wait a minute. Libraries are changing rapidly. With the onset of online databases, computerized catalogs, information on videodiscs and terminals, the advent of the electronic library, why teach people how to use libraries now? Aren't books and magazines on their way out? Won't anyone be able to find whatever information one wants just by dialing up, or simply by punching a few keys and communicating with a terminal?

To be sure, libraries are changing rapidly. What libraries (or whatever they'll be called) will look like in 2090, no one can predict. But if we only talk about the next generation—say the next fifteen or twenty years—we have a pretty good idea of what libraries will be like, which is probably not that different from what they are today. There will still be books and periodicals, but the big difference will be the amount and kinds of information that will be available even in the smallest, most isolated library, information that will be made available by new storage technologies, by new means of telecommunication, and by the next generation of computers. It will mean, almost literally, that any library anywhere will be able to provide its clientele with any printed or pictorial information they want. Moreover, with developments in artificial intelligence and expert systems, developments that are still in their infancy today, individuals will be able to search for such information much more efficiently and effectively.

Why then, should we spend time and energy now teaching our users how to make better use of our resources?

The most obvious response is that while information seekers fifteen years from now will have all sorts of electronic assistance to provide them with whatever information they need or want, in the meantime most users will still need the kinds of instruction we're giving them now. Just as the amount of information is increasing, so are society's needs to gain access to it, and to evaluate it. There are, in other words, any number of persons who need our assistance now and will continue to need it until our services are replaced, to an extent anyway, by the new information technology.

A second response, perhaps not nearly as apparent, is that the electronic assistance which will replace much of the personal-user instruction we now spend time on—the so-called "expert system"—will be based on the methods and procedures we're using and improving now. Expert systems, after all, are simply (to put it in very basic terms) a computer-based replication of a human expert's method and procedure. The better we're able to hone our user instruction skills now and the more precisely we can agree on what are the best methods and procedures, the more effective will be the expert systems that will eventually replace much of what we do now.

Not if, but when, much of what we do is replaced by technology, what will our role be? Our role, it seems to me, will be much the same as it is now, but on a very different level. In other words, where today we provide all levels of instruction, much of it basic group instruction, in years to come we will give more personalized help and let technology take care of basic needs. Librarians will act as information advisors, with responsibilities not unlike those of the traditional readers' advisors. Readers' advisory service grew out of the need to give users individual attention—not so much for answering specific questions or supplying particular information as for giving advice, generally on what the individual might like to read. Now we'll be advising on approaches to information, helping users shape search strategies, sort their information, and evaluate their sources.

The basic thrust of library instruction is to help our clientele make more effective use of our libraries' resources. That will not change. The resources available will be much greater in quantity, in variety, and in place of origin, but that will make expert, personal assistance even more essential. What we're doing now to help our clientele is commendable and important and it can provide the framework for our task over the next decades and for those who follow us beyond that.

Libraries and Information Literacy

May Brottman
Media Specialist
Glenbrook North High School
Northbrook, Illinois

Since the beginning of 1989, three reports have been issued that emphasize the need for "information literate people ... those who have learned how to learn." They are *Final Report of the American Library Association Presidential Committee on Information Literacy*, *The Nation's Report Card. Crossroads in American Education: A Summary of Findings*, and *Critical Thinking: Theory, Research, Practice, and Possibilities*. A person who is information literate is defined as one who is "able to recognize when information is needed and has the ability to locate, evaluate, and use effectively the needed information." (*Final Report*, 2) Thus, information literacy and the ability to learn have been related to a knowledge of the organization, scope, sources, and use of information.

However, in two of the three reports—*The Nation's Report Card* and *Critical Thinking*—the central source of information that is an important element in developing and exercising these necessary skills and abilities is omitted, namely libraries and librarians. And yet, to achieve this kind of literacy requires a good dose of educational experiences that enhance the knowledge and skills that are introduced in the classroom. The independent search for information in a curricular related task strengthens the organization, location, evaluation, and synthesizing skills learned in the classroom. To insure effective, progressive experiences that build these practical and critical thinking skills requires the continuous involvement of librarians, teachers, and faculty at all levels working cooperatively to develop and implement learning experiences that involve students independently using many of the information sources available in libraries and in the community. To enable students and lifelong learners to pursue information literacy calls for libraries to develop instructional programs that will first, engender information access skills, a prerequisite to pursuing independent inquiry, and second, involve the library faculty and staff working cooperatively with both users and other individuals, offices, and catalysts within their organization and community.

Given the emphasis on test scores at both the elementary and secondary level and the general reluctance of classroom teachers to forfeit their role as suppliers of information that helps students do well on these standardized tests, library programs that are not integrated into the entire school curriculum get lost by the wayside. Librarians who succeed in developing programs in cooperation with classroom teachers often find that the library learning experiences they provide for students are not repeated throughout the school year and thus are isolated exercises that have little carry-over between disciplines from year to year. As a result, library programs often fail to play a crucial role in the education of students not only in the primary and secondary schools, but also in higher education and beyond.

In the preface to *Critical Thinking*, Jonathan D. Fife sounds the lament that "since critical thinking is generally not encouraged at the elementary and secondary level, it becomes a central responsibility for higher education" (xv). To develop problem solving and critical thinking skills really requires exposure to various opinions, positions, rhetoric, and media, which can only be found in a variety of sources. And, in turn, locating, analyzing, and synthesizing material entail some level of critical thinking and problem solving skills. If students are to evolve into critical thinkers and information literate citizens, they must be made aware of the burgeoning sources for information and, more importantly, they must be given frequent opportunities to search for and use information to fulfill their assignments. Only regular, incremental exposure to the research process will prevent students from being overwhelmed and alienated by the mushrooming array of information sources.

A vital step in the process of developing a curriculum for critical thinking is to identify the skills necessary for accessing and evaluating information at each developmental level. Once the skills have been identified, the next step is to determine learning experiences to be introduced and elaborated on, so that throughout their schooling, students are continually building on previous information and critical thinking skills and engaging in more sophisticated experiences. To initiate specific skills without first determining the most effective time and the best experiences for reinforcing the learned skills creates a situation we now face—educational programs requiring information literacy skills that are not consistently used, understood, or retained. To effectively identify the skills and develop an articulated curriculum that is based on solid knowledge requires a rethinking of library instruction programs and the curricular experiences necessary at each level to introduce and reinforce access skills.

Instruction programs in all types of libraries should ideally be based on an overall, articulated plan that has identified needed skills at all levels and been developed by educators representing the range of education. This information literacy curriculum would require librarians to develop integrated programs of instruction and to take a proactive role in teaching information literacy to all members of the society. Instruction on such a scale needs a structured process to achieve both program specific goals and articulation with other programs. Consistency in the organization of individual programs will help provide a framework for the eventual development of an articulated curriculum at all levels and among all types of libraries. The purpose of this handbook is to promote such solid, well-planned programs.

Increased cooperation among administrators and teaching and library staff is a key ingredient to change. According to Bob McClure, Project Director of the NEA Mastery in Learning Project Staff, there is no differentiation in those schools involved with the project between librarians and other members of the faculty or staff. In many instances librarians are taking a leadership role in restructuring the school curriculum, and the library facilities and staff are organized as an integral part of the total educational process. In those institutions where there is no such coordinated planning, the first step would be to create a library instruction facility to accommodate an information literacy program and to generate interest among colleagues and other contacts.

Another key factor in developing information literate citizens is to truly engage students in learning. This requires restructuring the educational process to actively involve students in their own education. As the Educational Testing Service's report, *The Nation's Report Card. Crossroads in American Education*, emphasized in February 1989:

> For ... qualitatively different gains to occur [in higher levels of performance], the goals of instruction need to be reconsidered.... Educational theory and research suggest a different pattern of generative teaching and learning, where learning content and procedures and how to use this learning for specific purposes occur interactively. Students learn information, rules, and routines while learning to think about how these operate in the context of particular goals and challenges in their own lives. When students engage in activities that require them to use new learning, both their knowledge of content and skills and their ability to use them develop productively together. (40)

Libraries and resource centers are certainly one of the logical vehicles for the relevant instructional experiences that recent critics of American education hope will spur information literacy, critical thinking, and problem solving abilities. As both a source of information and an arena for information skills training, libraries have a very important role to play, but it will require the active involvement of librarians across the spectrum of institutions and communities. A first priority is to understand the information needs of users and to develop an articulated library instructional program. Well-designed, curriculum-related library instruction is an important link to information literacy, to empowering people to learn on their own.

WORKS CITED

Applebee, Arthur, Judith A. Langer, and Ina V. S. Mullis. *The Nation's Report Card. Crossroads in American Education: A Summary of Findings*. Princeton, N.J.: Educational Testing Service, 1989. (Report No: 17-OV-01)

Final Report. Chicago: American Library Association, Presidential Committee on Information Literacy, 1989.

Kurfiss, Joanne G. *Critical Thinking: Theory, Research, Practice and Possibilities*. (ASHE-ERIC Higher Education Report No. 2, 1988.) Washington, D.C.: Association for the Study of Higher Education, 1988.

Developing Programs in Library Use Instruction for Lifelong Learning
An Overview

Mary Loe
Coordinator of Library Instruction
Penfield Library
State University College of New York
Oswego, New York

Betsy Elkins
Coordinator of Public Services
Moon Library
SUNY College of Environmental Science and Forestry
Syracuse, New York

INTRODUCTION

Without a doubt this is an information age. People are producing and seeking more information on more topics and in more forms of media than ever before. Those who can locate and use information have a decided advantage over those who cannot. In fact, a rather alarming gap has developed between those who should know how to find information and those who actually do, and the concern for library literacy is growing.

Libraries, as a major source of information, are by necessity more complex than ever. Librarians and other information specialists may take this for granted, yet users seeking information can often be intimidated by the new technology for accessing that material. They are easily overwhelmed by the amount of information, its diverse format, storage, and methods of retrieval. As a result, librarians are no longer caretakers and conservators of information and knowledge alone; as information specialists they must be active facilitators and educators as well.

A good collection is the core of any library. However, the true measure of quality is how well a library collection is used. If library users are unable to effectively and efficiently gain access to the information they need, the library has failed in its mission.

From the eager child looking for a story in the public library to the retired personal investor checking current stock prices, people have information needs throughout their lives. Education is not a process completed at standard intervals in life. People begin to learn early and continue throughout their lives in a variety of settings and for a host of reasons. Though the realization of lifelong learning is as old as the perennial search for "the good life," it is also as new as the ongoing information revolution. The rapid changes in technology now require people to acquire new skills and have access to more information faster than ever before. This, in turn, has prompted more attention to lifelong learning and adult learners (Knowles; "Lifelong Learning"; *World Yearbook*). To accommodate this growing phenomenon, librarians in all kinds of libraries need to teach the use of libraries and demystify their information sources.

Such a Promethean task requires a great deal of coordination and communication among all those in the library profession. The policy statement from the American Library Association places the message clearly before us:

In order to assist individuals in the independent information retrieval process basic to daily living in a democratic society, the American Library Association encourages all libraries to include instruction in the use of libraries as one of the primary goals of service. Libraries of all types share the responsibility to educate users in successful information location, beginning with their childhood years and continuing the education process throughout their years of professional and personal growth. (ALA Policy Manual, 52.6—Instruction in the Use of Libraries)

Library instruction is not a recent idea—it has been practiced in schools for many years. However, in the last decade, it has received renewed interest in both academic institutions and in the library profession. Thus, all kinds and sizes of libraries have instituted programs because their staffs realized the increasing importance of educated use of the collections. What is still needed is collaboration among the types of libraries to develop full, well-articulated instruction programs.

The terms used in professional literature to describe the process of educating library users can be confusing. Library instruction, instruction in library use, and user education are all used to describe the teaching activities of a library. Library orientation commonly refers to any program or part of a program whose primary purpose is to acquaint the user with the physical layout and services of a library. Bibliographic instruction (BI) is the more intensive process of teaching library research methodology and searching skills. While BI teaches the use of specific bibliographic tools in a library, it is also sometimes used to describe general library instruction. Whatever it is called in print or in various libraries, "cradle to grave" instruction has become a permanent fact of library life, a requirement for the profession.

This chapter describes in general terms the common planning process that should take place when developing new library instruction programs or when reworking established programs in virtually any kind of library. Rationales for each step and definitions of terms are provided. The chapters that follow focus on the planning procedures for the different types of libraries in more specific detail and include planning forms and sample instructional materials.

PLANNING: DECIDING WHAT SHOULD AND CAN BE DONE

Assessing Needs

The process of developing programs in library use is not unlike the research process which is often taught in school, academic, public, and professional libraries. A logical, step-by-step strategy should be carefully followed to maximize success in both cases.

The first step in planning any instruction program is to thoroughly examine the current and projected needs of the specific library and its entire community. Just as a clearly defined topic makes a literature search easier, a carefully conducted needs assessment facilitates the rest of the planning program. A needs assessment is simply gathering data about what is already happening in library instruction and comparing this to what present and potential library users would like to have happen. This step is an evaluation of the library's actual world compared to its ideal. It insures that the library is responding to *real* rather than assumed needs of its users and provides the beginning road map for the rest of the planning trip. Both informal and formal methods are involved.

There are a number of ways to assess a library's needs informally. Simple observation of the reference desk is a good place to begin. Do patterns show up in the questions that are asked or who is asking them? Looking at statistics, studying internal library reports, and talking with library colleagues also provide information about the current instruction situation. Informal discussions with library users and nonusers concerning their information needs or research problems should be helpful as well.

A more formal needs assessment might involve personal interviews, documents analysis, and a survey mailed to representative members of the entire library community, nonusers as well as current patrons. A questionnaire can provide invaluable information about the actual instruction needs of the different kinds of library users. In order to get a good rate of return the questionnaire must be carefully constructed, brief, logical, devoid of library jargon, and at an appropriate reading level. All surveys should be pretested with people not already familiar with the library, but comparable to the library's target audience.

Some libraries will also want to include a study of their community's social and economic situation and environment (lifestyle, education, geography, resources, etc.) in their needs assessment. Institutional and local government planning offices can be of great assistance. Reviewing data such as current census reports and projections for the future can help one to understand the population which uses (and might use) a library and to determine its instructional needs.

While reviewing the needs of library users it is always important to examine instruction in light of the library's purposes and mission as well. Where does the library fit within the community, institution, or organization it serves? Assess any library instruction that may already be in place (lectures, tours, signs, printed material, computer help screens, etc.) and compare this to what should be done (what the users need).

Instruction should be compatible with, and support the mission of, the community it serves.

Patricia Breivik advocates the use of a matrix to identify user groups and determine their priorities (41). She suggests listing all possible user groups down the side of a page, and all possible instruction needs (e.g., orientation, basic skills, advanced subject matter, etc.) across the top of the page. Be creative at this point, attempting to include every possibility you can think of. This matrix arrangement can help identify areas of high need and may also suggest a sequential order for the learning experiences.

It is important to solicit help throughout this first stage of planning and needs assessment. In addition to chapters and bibliographies in this handbook, other current professional literature should prove useful. Discover what is happening in other libraries' situations: What is successful? What tends to fail? What trends are afoot? Keep in mind that every library is unique and ideas must be modified to suit an individual library.

Networking with other librarians can be one of the most inspiring and productive ways of gathering information. Visit similar libraries where programs are in place and talk with those involved (the users as well as the librarians). Attend some of the many conferences on instruction and contact regional and national library organizations. Standards for library skills and coordinated, sequential instruction can develop only from an ongoing exchange of professional experiences.

The Library Instruction Round Table (LIRT) of the American Library Association, which produced this handbook, provides a forum for communication among instruction librarians. Many states have similar groups within their state organizations, for example, the Library User Education Roundtable (LUERT) of the New York Library Association. The Library Orientation/Instruction Exchange (LOEX) located at Eastern Michigan University in Ypsilanti, Michigan, operates an invaluable national clearinghouse of planning and teaching materials which may be borrowed. LOEX also acts as a referral service that can put specific librarians in touch with one another and publishes an excellent quarterly newsletter on instruction, the *LOEX NEWS*. Each May a national library instruction conference is sponsored by LOEX. While the original focus of LOEX was academic libraries, it has broadened its concerns to instruction issues and activities in school, special, and public libraries as well.

A number of states have established their own library instruction clearinghouses. Like LOEX, these regional centers seek to provide a means of disseminating instruction information and materials. A Clearinghouse Committee within the Association of College and Research Libraries section (ACRL) of the American Library Association aims to facilitate cooperation and exchange among regional and state bibliographic instruction groups. This committee prepared the *Bibliographic Instruction Handbook* (1979), which is available from the ALA office in Chicago.

At any juncture in planning and implementing library instruction programs, colleagues and clearinghouses will be happy to share instruction materials, evaluation and assessment tools, information, and advice. For special problems, such as analyzing a library's unique data, it is wise to consider the use of consultants or experts in data collection and analysis.

Carrying out a needs assessment is time consuming, yet well worth the effort. It is the important first step which determines what library needs should be addressed. Without this hard information, choosing goals and workable objectives and selecting appropriate teaching techniques are no better than guesswork.

Developing General Goals

Whether the aim is to establish a new program, develop a new dimension, or improve an existing program, general goals and objectives are critical to planning and implementation. Once the library's population has been analyzed in the needs assessment, the next step is to work out an overall program which matches the needs of that population. Most likely a number of user groups and instruction needs have been identified, and goals and objectives should be developed accordingly.

Goals are general statements of purpose that give direction to subsequent planning details. General goals state the desired long-term outcomes of instruction. All libraries, regardless of type, will have some similar instruction goals such as: (1) to enable users to locate the information they need effectively and efficiently, or (2) to develop the user's ability to select and evaluate appropriate materials. General instruction goals must, however, also be meaningful to the particular needs of the user groups and attainable by the library. From these broad goals more specific goals and objectives will be written to indicate the desired outcomes (i.e., the behavior changes) which should result from the instruction. How to write these specific goals and objectives for particular programs will be explored later in this chapter.

General Administration and Staff Support

Instruction programs can grow out of a number of library situations. A group of patrons might request instruction of a specific nature. Library staff members may sense a need for special help and begin to develop a program in response. The administration of an organization, realizing that patrons need more attentive help, might decide that a formal instruction program is the answer. The best impetus for library instruction, of course, is the combined interest and support of all parties.

Throughout the planning process it is imperative to keep lines of communication open. Working through proper channels and keeping the instruction planning activities visible can be critical. Since support of the library director, trustees, administration, or whoever controls the library is vital to the success of any library instruction program, lack of strong administrative support will hobble even the best designed program. Time, money, personnel, and facilities are required for library instruction; the administration controls all these. The good will and interest of the librarian(s), support staff, and

possibly other colleagues is equally essential, for in the end the success of the program depends on those who carry it out. To gain this support, positive and realistic plans, justified by overall goals, must be presented to everyone affected by the proposed program, and the results of the needs assessment should be shared.

Administrators, trustees, or supervisors may need to be convinced of the importance of library instruction: How will it enhance library service and use? How might it improve library public relations? Describe what the library audience can gain from library instruction: training in specific research methods, an awareness of the complexity of information systems, as well as confidence in using them. The effectiveness of group instruction over individual instruction at the reference desk might also be viewed as an asset.

Grass roots support from the library staff and other key individuals is equally important, whether within a single library or throughout organizations like school districts or cities with branch libraries. All staff members, especially those who will be carrying out and supporting the instruction, should be included in the process of planning the program and sensitized as to how it will help the entire library and its constituents. Consider the social and political context of change in any institution and the implications of change in the particular library's milieu. Librarians may need a persuasive and sympathetic leader. If instruction has not been perceived as part of the librarians' professional duties in the past, the transition may take time. Group instruction and teaching evaluations are intimidating to many people. Plans should be made to ensure that training and assistance is available when needed.

The quality and quantity of administrative and staff support will ultimately dictate what the final instruction program will be. Despite the loftiest of goals, there are some given limitations which need to be considered. Staff and budget will prove the bottom line in any instruction program. Once the ideal goals are set, they need to be checked against the real library world to ensure that there are enough resources and time to accomplish these goals. From the internal and external data gathered so far, informed decisions can be made. It may be necessary to start the library instruction program on a very small, piecemeal basis. Or, it may be that the primary instruction goals are not unrealistic after all and are largely attainable. Encouraged, planners should proceed to the next stage: the design and implementation of a particular instruction program.

DEVELOPING A SPECIFIC LIBRARY INSTRUCTION PROGRAM

The design of a specific library instruction program depends on its particular audience, its target group. Often the first planning step, the needs assessment, identifies more than one segment of a library's community or constituency that would benefit from instruction in information searching. Which instructional program to focus on first depends on the library's general goals, its existing programs, and available resources, especially staff. Whether the choice is to initiate an instruction program for a library's entire audience, alter an existing program, or address the needs of a specialized segment of patrons such as small business owners, the traits of the selected program audience should be carefully considered.

Analyzing the Program's Audience

An understanding of the program's projected participants is essential to setting realistic objectives and planning learning activities that can successfully engage that targeted audience. Consider the group's characteristics and how homogeneous it is. Age, maturity, previous library experience, information needs, and learning styles invariably affect program design. So does the size of the population. The group's attitudes towards libraries, its ease of access to the library, and its language proficiency are other important variables. The profile that results from this population analysis provides the basis for subsequent program decisions: What ought to be learned? How can it best be taught? When, where, and how should the learning take place?

Stating Specific Goals: The Program's Purpose

The larger goal of any library instruction program is to improve the way people go about finding information. The goals of a particular instruction program state more specific purposes for that program and give direction to more detailed planning. To function as guidelines, goals should be carefully delineated at the start with realistic expectations for the special audience in mind. It is also not too early to start considering possible evaluation methods, since the program's effectiveness will be measured against its specific goals. A number of goals may be identified for a given program, depending on the vantages of all parties involved. For example, a single instruction program could be developed to: (1) promote library use among a group of potential patrons, (2) decrease anxieties about using the library's online systems, (3) justify the purchase of a very expensive service, and (4) enhance the library's image within the community or business.

Setting Objectives

Objectives are derived directly from the program goals, but state systematically the desired outcome of the instructional program in much more specific terms. The time and discipline required for setting instructional objectives are well spent, because clearly defined objectives answer several vital questions for both the instructor and the audience: What is to be taught and learned? How is teaching and learning to be achieved? Exactly how can the learning be demonstrated? Written objectives also give credence to the instruction program and can be invaluable in gaining administrative or outside grant support for the program.

Establishing the specific objectives helps ensure that a program's content and instruction suit the needs, abilities, and attitudes of the target audience. The process also helps avoid what is the most common flaw in library instruction: trying to cover too much material. Most library instruction is carried out within severe time constraints, and it is a constant temptation to pack more information into that time frame than can be effectively learned. Clear objectives are especially useful if several librarians share responsibility for a program and need reasonable assurance that they are teaching the same thing. The program's audience benefits from knowing clearly and concretely what is expected of and for them. And finally, good objectives set the stage for program evaluation.

Instructional objectives are variously called behavioral objectives, performance objectives, or enabling objectives. These terms emphasize behavior because they describe observable skills or actions that should result from the learning experience. Though there is strong agreement that meaningful objectives must be written in terms of desired changes in behavior, it is also important to recognize the implicit value of cognitive and affective objectives. Library instruction is usually meant to encourage understanding and knowledge of particular library tools (a cognitive objective), and it is hoped that patrons will feel comfortable about using those tools after the learning experience (an affective objective). Since cognitive and affective changes are hard to measure in themselves, the behavior that is indicative of such learning is best stated as performance or enabling objectives.

A formula for constructing performance objectives is given by Janet L. Freedman and Harold A. Bantley (18):

$$\text{Performance Objective} = \\ \text{Task} + \text{Conditions} + \text{Standards.}$$

The task is the observable action; conditions are the situation within which the task is carried out; and when standards are appropriate, they indicate criteria such as accuracy and speed. If this makes the articulation of performance objectives seem easy, be forewarned. Clear, concise language must be used. To be most direct, objectives should be simple (not compound) and written in active verb tense with the patron as the subject. For example: The patron will interpret a citation in ... To be sure that performance objectives are clear and observable, test them on both colleagues and patrons.

Examples of performance objectives may help clarify the formula:

- After reading the point-of-use instruction for *The New York Times Index*, patrons will identify and correctly interpret a reference in the index.

- All paralegals in the organization will complete three successful, solo searches on Lexis after participating in this six-lesson workshop.

- Given a topic, the patron will accurately identify three books in the library catalog on that topic.

Full sets of model objectives are included in the ACRL *Bibliographic Instruction Handbook*. Look for additional and more elaborate examples of objectives in sections of this handbook for the different types of libraries.

Selecting Teaching Methods

With the selected audience and specific objectives clearly in mind, it is time to consider the array of possible instructional methods and their combinations. Very often several teaching methods together help promote the desired objectives. No one method is likely to loom forth as the best to use, but some methods can be self eliminating. Tutorials, for example, are clearly a poor choice if the goal is for one librarian to reach an audience of 200. Public library patrons are likely to require a type of instruction that allows flexible scheduling. In schools, class assignments are the vehicle for learning to use libraries and information, so attention to the design and execution of assignments may best promote library instruction. Useful charts for quickly analyzing the pros and cons of the various teaching modes have been developed by Anne K. Beaubien, et al. (figure 1.1). The modes range from point-of-use explanations to formal courses and are appropriate for any type of library.

The most important factors that affect the choice of teaching methods are (1) staff interest, abilities, and experience, (2) the size of the intended audience, (3) the time available to both librarians and their audience for instruction, (4) the nature and level of instruction planned, (5) requirements for equipment and facilities, and (6) the time and costs involved in revising program materials for continued use. As Beaubien et al. make clear, these factors are viewed differently from various perspectives (62). Administrators need to be concerned with cost-effectiveness, staff preparation, and public relations, whereas the staff must also consider time constraints, the learning objectives, scheduling, and their own skills. Patrons tend to prefer methods that are available when needed, easy, and efficient. In practice, the chosen teaching style usually employs several methods and such combinations often provide a better learning experience than any single method.

	PROS	CONS
Printed Materials		
General (Information sheets, how to find..., how to use..., self-guided tour)	Can cover orientation topics	Seldom convey question analysis, search strategy, discipline growth, nature of types of tools, bibliographic structure, or transferability to other topics or disciplines.
	Effectively convey a specific tool	
	Available to users all hours the library is open	
	User does not have to ask for help	Not flexible to user needs
	Could complement a class	User may conclude this is everything
	Once prepared, saves constant repetition of core information	User must be motivated to use
		Might not be used
	Relatively inexpensive to produce	May need copyright permission
	Relatively easily updated	Difficult to evaluate effectiveness
	Require little space to display	No librarian contact
	Do not need faculty or outside approval	
	Reach a wide audience	
	Good advertising for the library	
	Can place in freshman packet or send to other user groups	
Bibliographies and discipline guides	In addition to above:	In addition to above:
	Can explain the concept of types of tools	Provide little guidance unless annotated
	Can be subject specific or format specific	
	Are readily adaptable one library to another	
	Provide tools selected by professionals	

	PROS	CONS
Pathfinders	In addition to above: Convey a search strategy to follow Are efficient for users Commercially available with possibilities for local adaptations	In addition to above: Topics are necessarily narrow, so many needed to reach all groups of users
Audiovisual Presentations (videotape, audiotape, film, slide/tape)	Can cover orientation topics Can effectively explain a specific tool, the process of question analysis, and the nature of a type of tool Can combine orientation and instruction Available when needed User does not have to ask for help Could complement a class Once prepared, saves constant repetition of core information Can make multiple copies for showing in different locations Do not need outside approval Repeatable Commercially available	Seldom convey search strategy, growth of discipline, bibliographic structure, or transferability to other topics or disciplines Not flexible to user needs Must be high quality to compete with expectations built up by commercial television User may be embarrassed to use Some people intimidated by AV equipment Might not be used May need copyright permission (especially for background music) Require many technical skills Equipment is expensive and requires expert maintenance Need considerable space, outlets, special lighting Difficult to evaluate effectiveness
Point-of-use Explanations (printed or AV)	Effectively conveys a tool, nature of types of tools, and orientation Available all hours the library is open User does not have to ask for help Could complement a class as a transparency or handout Once prepared, saves constant repetition of core information User can reread or repeat as often as necessary for comprehension Do not need faculty or outside approval Commercially available with possibilities for local adaptations Reach a wide audience	Seldom convey question analysis, search strategy, growth of a discipline, bibliographic structure, or transferability to other topics or disciplines Difficult to keep detailed and concise User must find the tool first Not flexible to user needs User must be motivated User may be embarrassed to use Some people intimidated by AV equipment Might not be used May require valuable space Difficult to evaluate effectiveness

(Figure 1.1 continues on p. 12.)

	PROS	CONS
Programmed Instruction		
(workbooks or computer-assisted modules)	Can convey concepts of types of tools, a specific tool, search strategy, and question analysis	Seldom convey question analysis, growth of a discipline, bibliographic structure, or transferability to other topics or disciplines
	Available when needed	Often based on discrete bits of information rather than broad concepts
	Done at user's own pace and convenience	User must be motivated
	User does not have to ask for help	Not flexible to user needs
	Immediate reinforcement of progress	Time-consuming to prepare initially
	Can utilize a unique set of questions	Must be carefully pretested
	Could complement a course	Require revision
	Reach a wide audience	Tools containing answers will wear out faster
	Commercially available with possibilities for local adaptations	
	Evaluation built in	Also, for CAI:
		Users must be trained to work the machine
		User may not play with a system
		Instruction is not portable
		Computers have downtime
		Some programs do not require handling of reference tools
		Specialized programmer required
		Equipment is expensive and requires expert maintenance
		Computer time is expensive
Single Lectures		
	Convey concept of types of tools, question analysis, search strategy, growth of a discipline, bibliographic structure, or a specific tool	Seldom convey transferability to other topics or disciplines
	Flexible pace for user needs	Motivation is slow unless there is an assignment or innate interest
	Tailored to user level	Require teaching skills
	Allows personal interaction between librarian and user	Require many repetitions to reach total audience
	Librarian is visible in library's community	Time-consuming to prepare initially
	Reach a relatively wide audience	Scheduling problems with librarians' time
	Repeatable with modifications	May require creation of teaching space in library
	Can be course-related or course-integrated for trainees, students, etc.	If course integrated, need cooperation outside the library
		Difficult to evaluate effectiveness

	PROS	CONS
Formal Courses		
	Can teach search strategy, growth of a discipline, bibliographic structure, a specific tool, the process of question analysis, the nature of a type of tool, or transferability to other topics or disciplines	Users could become dependent on librarian
		Require teaching skills
		Require curriculum design skills
	Reinforcement of learning possible through exercises, projects, etc.	In academic setting, need formal approval
		Scheduling problems with librarians' time
	Tailored to user needs and pace	Time-consuming to prepare initially
	Allow personal interaction between librarian and user	
	Librarian is visible in library's community	
	Team teaching possible	
	Flexible after initial preparation	
	Evaluation easily incorporated	
Tutorials		
	Can convey types of tools, a specific tool, question analysis, search strategy, growth of a discipline, bibliographic structure, and transferability to other topics or disciplines	Users could become dependent on librarian
		Require interpersonal teaching skills
		Require in-depth discipline knowledge
	Can be given when needed	Scheduling problems with librarians' time
	Based on user's own needs	Very limited audience
	Allow personal interaction between librarian and user	Very time consuming
	Allow instant feedback	
	Level of sophistication readily adjusted	
	No special space or equipment is needed	
	No faculty involvement needed in academic setting	

Fig. 1.1. Modes of bibliographic instruction: Pros and cons. The original version of this table appeared in *Bibliographic Instruction Handbook*, Policy and Planning Committee, Bibliographic Instruction Section (Chicago: ACRL, ALA, 1979), pp. 46-55.

Developing Curriculum

The program's curriculum, that is its content and learning activities, should be derived directly from the needs assessment. If the targeted audience does not really need or want to learn what the program offers, the program will simply not work. Everything that is taught should support at least one of the written instructional objectives, and no objective should be left unmatched to specific content. Even with written objectives to help limit the program's content, however, librarians need to be careful in determining what to include. Breivik does not exaggerate the danger of overkill and the need for "Ruthlessness ... at this point" (83). If particular information is not essential for achieving one of the objectives, leave it out.

So cautioned, however, librarians still struggle with all they have to offer. It is rarefied library instruction that focuses purely on research sources. Basic content considerations usually include library procedures and logistics, audience attitudes and preconceptions, search strategies, the organization of information (within the library, within the community, within particular disciplines, etc.), and resources that may or may not be subject specific. Practical information about the library will always be essential to a greater or lesser degree, but the content should focus on the specific needs of the audience at a level that dovetails with its experience. If the original needs assessment does not provide sufficient information about a particular audience's library skills and experience, a brief, presession survey or pretest may be able to fill the gap.

Learning activities that can be used in library instruction include the whole gamut of ideas used in other arenas of education. These approaches and materials are related to the teaching methods chosen and the program's content. Look over the range of activities and techniques described in other sections of this handbook, as well as in other sources, and do not be afraid to experiment. In particular, consider ways to involve the audience, since it is well known that learning is retained best when information is heard, seen, and then used in practice. Peer teaching in pairs, for example, can solve a problem when half of a class is familiar with a source and the other half needs to be, and such a workshop may be far more efficient and effective than either a slide presentation or a detailed lecture. The heady growth of CD-ROM products and their variants is drawing new attention to research skills and readily offers library instructors the chance to tap users' curiosity and engage them in interactive sessions.

Much of the literature on library instruction deals with teaching techniques and methods, so plenty of models are available. Carolyn Kirkendall, the director of LOEX, reported a decline in queries for "new," experimental instruction samples at the end of the 1970s, presumably because participants have discovered that the best instruction techniques and materials are not necessarily innovative (31). Lectures, games, handouts, bibliographies, guides—whatever librarians use as the vehicle of their content—the main rule is to keep them short and simple, and geared always to the preestablished objectives.

PRACTICAL CONSIDERATIONS

Managing and Staffing the Program

Any aspect of a library instruction program that requires continuity or liaison effort needs management. How day-to-day administration is handled can vary greatly depending on program staff and size. In a small library, instruction can be yet another task the sole librarian adds to all of the other professional duties. In a large library, a full-fledged instruction program might be handled by a specialized, separate unit supervised by one or more librarians. Given the initial financial and administrative support necessary to bring even a small scale program to this stage of development, someone must now be responsible for nurturing and maintaining the program.

The two most common deterrents to instruction programs reported by librarians in all kinds of libraries are lack of interest outside the library and insufficient staff (Surveys). Although these are disturbingly real problems, they do not need to nip library instruction programs in the bud. Rather, these constraints argue for modes of instruction that are least labor intensive and the careful promotion of every small success achieved by the program. To get off the ground and to stay alive, instruction programs need initiators, adventurers, and planners. Especially where interest and support for library instruction is slowly garnered, it is vital that someone keep the big picture before trustees, managers, or administrators, and maintain hard-won contacts over the flux of years.

For programs that involve more than a few librarians, a major administrative task is to identify staffing needs and help select and train the staff. Staff development is often an ongoing necessity because of personnel turnover and program changes. For anything more than a very small operation, creating a pool of library instructors who share responsibilities is beneficial. The resulting increased professional interaction and visibility are enhancing to most librarians, the program, and the library. If several librarians are involved with instruction, new staff can take the time to be initiated slowly; develop their own teaching skills, style, and confidence; and gradually take on more specialized or heavier responsibilities. Library instructors definitely benefit from being able to share their experiences and work on common problems, and a team of instructors provides substitutes for the inevitable emergencies.

The two usual courses of action for creating such a pool of library instructors are: (1) to train interested current librarians and (2) to make instruction part of all new librarians' job descriptions. A combination of both tactics takes advantage of the ready interest of individual staff members, encourages the meek, and ensures new teaching strengths in various areas needed as a program develops.

To produce quality instruction programs and to develop as teachers, librarians must have the preparation time, the materials support, and some free reign for outreach efforts. Library instruction topics are frequently featured at conferences and workshops. Attendance at the regional or national level can be a valuable experience for both new and experienced library instructors and can stimulate improvements in the home library.

A staff issue that should not be overlooked is the need for support staff which is so often vital to a working program. The continual development of instruction materials, maintenance of equipment and facilities, making schedules, and keeping statistics are some of the clerical or paraprofessional tasks on which the entire program can rest. Often the library's institution can provide adequate help in many of these areas, but it is important to recognize in advance that a sufficient support staff will be needed to carry out these duties.

Additional Costs

Budgeting the overall library instruction program should be done during the early stages when library goals and objectives are set. With staffing and a budget line established, there are still costs that need to be considered. Equipment, publicity, and production of materials that stand up to high use and high standards can be expensive. A slide projector built for educational use, for example, costs considerably more than a standard model. Computer-assisted instruction has strong advantages for group instruction, but the initial cost is considerable. Computer graphics and laser printing allow libraries to create attractive, professional-looking guides, signs, and handouts, but can the library justify the purchase of such equipment if it's facing a budget cut? Expenses like these need not be a deterrent, however. The old standbys, blackboard and chalk, are always available. Modest supplies and equipment can be enough to start a small, well-planned program. And resourceful librarians may be able to find other avenues for borrowing or sharing equipment and materials.

Publicity

The goal of a given program will determine the audience, the amount, and the manner of the publicity. Some forms of instruction are self promoting. This is one chief advantage of point-of-use instruction. Other more formal instruction must be publicized because any chance for success depends upon convincing individuals and groups of the importance of improving their research skills.

For most libraries, professional contacts throughout the library's community or organization are invaluable conduits for spreading the word about a program. Send information to individuals, library friends groups, organizations, departments, and agencies that should be interested in the program, or that work with potential patrons. Use newsletters, send flyers, and make personal announcements whenever appropriate. Take advantage of coffee breaks and lunches to introduce and promote the program to key people.

Publicity to an audience at large can be placed in community centers, churches, and the library itself, and promotional copy should be sent to various media. Newspapers and radio stations regularly give space to public service announcements. Local television stations may make similar announcements or even be willing to do a special feature. Regular library

newspaper columns and other outreach work in a library's community can keep the library's general audience informed about the need for information searching skills and ways to acquire them. In every public communication, make sure that the promotional information is clear, accurate, and timely. No one wants to hear about an event after it has occurred.

Space to Work

An instruction program of any size requires space both for planning and delivering the instruction to library users. Working space must be adequate and a separate, designated instruction area with shelving, work tables, files, and storage space is ideal. Instruction materials, handouts, and equipment to be used should be housed in a readily available area. Well-designed display units are useful for distributing guides and other materials meant to be picked up by the public.

Adequate space to deliver instruction is an obvious need, but how to provide it is not always clear to libraries already outgrowing their four walls. A comfortable, well-equipped conference room or classroom adjacent to the reference area of the library is frequently the best situation. Specific tools can easily be brought to the room for workshops and classes can adjourn to the reference area of the library for lab exercises. The impact of group instruction on other patrons' use of the library should be a factor in considering where and when sessions take place. The space used for teaching should suit the size of the program and be equipped with adequate outlets and the necessary teaching aids — blackboard, chalk, overhead projectors, computers, telephone lines, or whatever the program needs.

There are situations when instruction within the library is not possible or even desirable. Certainly many instruction modes and materials are portable and work well in various surroundings. In every case, librarians should be familiar with the space in which they expect to function; it is poor planning and embarrassing to arrive with a slide show only to discover that a room can not be darkened.

Scheduling Library Use Instruction

The timing of instruction is important and should be dictated primarily by when the audience needs or can best use instruction. An influx of new members into the library community, an important new acquisition like an end-user database, and a new research project or class assignment are all occasions around which instruction could be scheduled. To be useful, formal instruction programs have to be offered at the time of the day, week, or year that is convenient to the targeted audience.

Whenever possible, staff preferences and priorities should also be factored into scheduling decisions. Patterns of library use are a third factor to consider. It is, for instance, counterproductive to schedule multiple classes to use the same index during the same hour. Quiet periods in a library's day, week or year may be appropriate times for scheduling instruction that might otherwise be too intrusive.

Starting Up: Take It Easy

After carefully planning the total instruction program, start implementing one or more of the various specific programs. If resources allow, it can be tempting to try everything at once, but starting small is the wiser approach. Choose a basic, important part of the total instruction plan and initiate a pilot program. This is an excellent way to test all of the planning and get more feedback while the program is still quite malleable. Small problems get ironed out and small successes are nourished into bigger ones. Once the pilot program is established, other dimensions can more easily be added.

Evaluation

Program evaluation is the systematic ongoing process of obtaining meaningful information in order to judge the merits of a program. Interest in evaluation has grown tremendously since the 1970s. The more recent emphasis on scientific methods helps account for the fact that while almost everyone agrees on the usefulness of evaluation, it tends to get overlooked or put aside for later. Regular appraisal is essential, however, both: (1) to improve an instruction program and (2) to determine how well its goal and objectives are being met. Evaluation results should also, of course, be used to support administrative decisions about maintaining and developing the program. It can be important to distinguish, however, between the two roles: the evaluator, who provides information, and the decision maker, who makes judgments based on that information. The context of evaluation always entails a political dimension. While evaluators should be realistic about this fact, they should also guard against losing their educator's perspective.

The questions that library instruction program evaluation can answer are: (1) Is the intended content learned? (2) Have the participants' research skills improved? (3) Was the instructor effective? (4) Have participants' attitudes towards library research and librarians changed? (5) Overall, is the program plan itself good?

From this last question it should be clear that the ideal time to start thinking of systematic evaluation is during the early planning stages when the purpose and objectives of the program are clarified. The needs assessment is really the first evaluative step that helps determine program objectives. Evaluation criteria derive from the program's objectives and are measured by its outcomes. Anticipation of evaluation requirements makes the designing of some evaluation instruments much easier. For instance, a test of a program's content or of changes in program participants' knowledge should always be based specifically on that program's instructional and performance objectives. If systematic evaluation was not developed along with the instruction program, time and care should be taken to ensure that evaluation procedures are developed and that they produce useful results.

Given the range of evaluation procedures, from experimental research design to cost-benefit studies, it is not surprising that different approaches have their own proponents. There is no one program evaluation model to follow. An eclectic approach that uses the strengths of research design as well as contextual and economic studies is often the best way to proceed.

In determining what evaluation techniques and instruments to use, first consider the purpose of the evaluation. Different types of evaluation typically occur at different stages of a program's development. Is the evaluation intended to guide the planning, implementation, or improvement of the program and instruction (formative evaluation)? Or, that is, is it meant to give a valid assessment of what has occurred, whether standards have been met (summative evaluation)? Then consider what kinds of methodologies, both formal and informal, are most suitable for the evaluation.

Formal Evaluation

The formal measurements of content, knowledge, and skills take preparation time and usually are appropriate for the more formal instruction modes: courses, workshops, and other serial sessions. Objective post-tests can quickly indicate cognitive retention of material covered in a program, but a comparison of post- and pretest scores or a control group is needed to ascertain what difference the instruction made. Longitudinal studies of users who complete certain library instruction programs would be useful to determine what long-term effects those programs have. Library exercises or worksheets are often used to give participants practice with particular information tools after being instructed in their use. This hands-on experience under the tutelage of a librarian helps make up for participants' different levels of understanding and weaknesses in the instruction, plus it gives a measure of performance.

To assess attitudes toward the program, survey questionnaires and rating scales can give feedback from participants or a planted observer, such as a colleague. These instruments are used in the vast majority of teacher evaluation procedures. Surveys are easy to administer, but they do require careful attention in order to yield useful and accurate data. The format of the instrument, its length, and dimensions to include must be considered. Questionnaires that use open-ended questions often provide the most interesting feedback, but the answers can be difficult to tally and compare. A question like "How could this program be improved?" needs an open-ended format to allow for a free flow of ideas. "Was the exercise useful?" is an example of a question that best suits a multiple choice form or a rating scale. The degrees of the respondents' favorable or unfavorable judgment are predetermined by the range provided in the survey, and therefore easily categorized. Since some aspects of programs are not readily reduced to measurable units, it is common practice to include one overall holistic assessment on rating surveys. Using both open-ended and scaled response questions combines the advantages of both types of surveys.

These formal surveys, tests, and exercises take time to administer but even more time to create. It is very important to field test any new instrument with several people to highlight possible problems. The questions must be clear and answers should be a true measurement of what is meant to be measured. Technical aspects of formal evaluation pose problems for many librarians unfamiliar with research design, questionnaire construction, data analysis, etc. (See figures 2.5, 2.6, and 2.7 on pp. 33-35 and appendix B on pp. 63-65.) Overviews on program evaluation by Harriet Talmadge and teacher evaluation by James Raths, various texts on research methods, local specialists in educational or psychological research, or an outside consultant can help in planning and making use of the results. A brief review of selected procedures and instruments with an expert can prevent wasted effort and piles of meaningless data.

Informal Evaluation

Informal methods of evaluation include the subjective ways we normally pick up information from people around us. During library instruction, for instance, participants communicate verbally and nonverbally whether they understand a term used or are puzzled about a concept. An unclear worksheet will prompt a flood of questions. By paying attention to these signals of confusion, comprehension, attentiveness, etc., the instructor can respond to problems and misunderstandings as they arise. This immediate feedback is the most valuable conduit for ideas on how to improve presentations and instructional materials.

Indirect feedback from other observers also filters back and can be an indicator of how well the instruction program is going. Such information need not be altogether casual and serendipitous. Ask individuals who are in positions to make observations—colleagues, teachers, other library staff—for evidence of changed attitudes and behavior. Have research practices improved? Did the instruction have positive or negative impact on other services in the library? Though informal methods of evaluation are by definition subjective, and therefore should not be the sole means of evaluation, they can give concrete and immediate feedback which is extremely useful to instructors and program planners.

The evidence from program evaluations and instruction statistics should be gathered and analyzed every year. Since its primary purpose is to encourage informed action, the practical use made of evaluations indicates the value of the study. Some of the findings will be useful for public relations purposes and required reports. Summarized in an annual report, the program trends, accomplishments, and current objectives can then be shared with all parties who should be kept informed about the instruction program's development. Instruction activities should also be kept in mind whenever other library research is carried out, such as library use studies.

The purpose of evaluation is to get relatively accurate answers to hard questions about the success and cost effectiveness of a program. Evaluators should be mindful of the limitations of any one methodology and alert to the educational and political content of their work. Program development implies change, preferably improvements. Without a doubt the flux of budgets and staffs can also require changes that do not enhance programs. With the information gathered throughout the stages of planning and implementing the library instruction program, librarians will be able to make sound decisions about how to best meet instruction goals within different cost considerations.

CONCLUSIONS

Selecting and organizing materials have always been the fundamental purpose of any library. Like reference service, library instruction in all its facets has come a long way from the initial "aid to readers" concept of the nineteenth century; it is a basic service of libraries in this fast-paced information age. Precisely how different libraries deliver this basic service will, of course, vary. Each library's situation—its goals, size, community/clientele, personnel, and resources—presents a unique milieu for library instruction. But the overall goal of a literate and information literate society and the way to generate a sound, useful library program are essentially the same. This chapter has presented an overview of the planning stages important for any library instruction program in any setting. The following chapters are more specific; they provide information and concrete examples for designing successful instruction programs in special, public, school, and academic libraries.

BIBLIOGRAPHY

"ALA Policy Manual, 52.6." In *ALA Handbook of Organization 1988/1989*. Chicago: American Library Association, 1988.

Beaubien, Anne K. et al. *Learning the Library*. New York: R. R. Bowker Company, 1982.

Breivik, Patricia. *Planning the Library Instruction Program*. Chicago: American Library Association, 1982.

Bibliographic Instruction Handbook. Chicago: American Library Association, Association of College and Research Libraries/Bibliographic Instruction Section, 1979.

Freedman, Janet L., and Harold A. Bantly. *Information Searching*. 2nd ed. Metuchen, N.J.: Scarecrow Press, 1982.

Gratch, Bonnie G. "Rethinking Instructional Assumptions in an Age of Computerized Information Access." *Research Strategies* 5 (Summer 1987): 4-7.

Kirkendall, Carolyn. "Library Use Education: Current Practices and Trends." *Library Trends* 29 (Summer 1980): 29-37.

Knowles, Malcolm. *The Adult Learner: A Neglected Species*. 2nd ed. Houston, Tex.: Gulf Publishing, 1979.

"Lifelong Learning: Changes in Social Skills." In *The International Encyclopedia of Education*. Oxford: Pergamon Press, 1985.

Raths, James. "Evaluation of Teachers." In *Encyclopedia of Educational Research*, 611-17. New York: Free Press, 1982.

Renford, Beverly, and Linnea Hendrickson. *Bibliographic Instruction: A Handbook*. New York: Neal-Schuman Publishers, Inc., 1980.

Roberts, Anne F. *Library Instruction for Librarians*. Littleton, Colo.: Libraries Unlimited, Inc., 1982.

Surveys by Type of Library. Unpublished surveys taken by the Handbook Committee, Library Instruction Round Table, American Library Association, 1985.

Talmadge, Harriet. "Evaluation of Programs." In *Encyclopedia of Educational Research*, 605-11. New York: Free Press, 1982.

World Yearbook of Education 1979: Recurrent Education and Lifelong Learning. London: Kogan Page, 1979.

PART II
ACADEMIC LIBRARIES

Library Instruction in Academic Libraries Including Graduate, Four-Year, and Two-Year Institutions

Sandy Ready
Mankato State University
Mankato, Minnesota

Marvin E. Wiggins
Brigham Young University
Provo, Utah

Sharon Stewart
University of Alabama
University, Alabama

Katherine Jordan
Northern Virginia Community College
Alexandria, Virginia

Kathy Sabol
Northern Virginia Community College
Manassas, Virginia

INTRODUCTION

The concept of library instruction in academic libraries is not new. College and university librarians have long accepted the notion that in addition to assisting users with the identification of specific needed information, they also have an obligation to demonstrate searching skills which could enable their users to function more independently. Each reference encounter should not only provide the information sought, but also explain *how* the information is located, encouraging users to replicate the process in the future without assistance.

Unfortunately, the constraints of time and staff frequently make this intense one-to-one encounter difficult, if not impossible. As the volume of available information grows and users demand access to a wider variety of sources, librarians find they are unable to devote the needed energy to each encounter. The solution to this dilemma is to provide a more formalized type of instruction where groups of users may be introduced to the sources and skills needed for their information searches.

Generally, library instruction can be divided into two smaller categories: library orientation and bibliographic instruction. As the name implies, library orientation is the steps taken to familiarize users with the physical arrangement of the library, its services, and its policies. Bibliographic instruction (BI) includes activities designed to teach about information resources and research techniques (Renford and Hendrickson, pp. 184-85). A well-developed library instruction program contains both orientation *and* instruction, and successful programs are based on careful planning *prior* to presentation.

The planning process includes:

- Assessment of instructional needs.
- Assessment of current activities.
- Development of program goals and instructional objectives.
- Selection of instructional methods.
- Evaluation of the program.

In addition, consideration should be given to:

- Staffing
- Budget
- Facilities
- Public relations
- Program support

ASSESSMENT OF INSTRUCTIONAL NEEDS

If the instruction program is to be successful, it is necessary to examine not only what users need to know in order to accomplish their information searches, but also what information librarians feel their users need in order for them to be more self-sufficient. A formal analysis of a library's public and a compilation of their needs is called a needs assessment. In 1979 the Policy and Planning Committee, Bibliographic Instruction Section of ALA's Association of College and Research Libraries prepared excellent guidelines for conducting a formal needs assessment for library-use instruction. The following has been adapted from their guidelines.*

---

*Adapted and reprinted by permission of the American Library Association from "Academic Section," *ACRL Bibliographic Instruction Handbook* (Chicago: American Library Association, 1979), 48-55.

The Academic Community

Those who make up the academic community include students, faculty, staff, administrators, and nonuniversity users (including other academic institutions and their clientele, libraries, and the geographical community).

Groups

A profile of information needs should begin with an understanding of the people and groups who make up the academic community. Figures on the size of these groups will lead to a preliminary understanding of the audience and assist in making procedural, instructional, and operational decisions. Different groups have differing needs and approaches to satisfying these needs should vary accordingly. The following data should be gathered even though it will not all be used initially, because the information will help to identify the total instructional needs of the institution and to highlight areas with which to begin.

1. Student characteristics

    A. Student profile: educational, socio-economic, cultural background (foreign born), and average age. A profile might be necessary for every class enrolled, including transfers and special programs; entrance test scores required for admission.

    B. Number of undergraduate students for each class enrolled.

    C. Number of graduate students

    D. Number of full-time students
       (1) Undergraduate
       (2) Graduate

    E. Number of part-time students
       (1) Undergraduate
       (2) Graduate

    F. Number of transfer students

    G. Enrollment by class and degree
       (1) Freshmen
       (2) Sophomores
       (3) Juniors
       (4) Seniors
       (5) Nondegree undergraduate
       (6) Master's
       (7) Doctoral
       (8) Professional
       (9) Nondegree graduate

    H. Enrollment by major or program
       (1) Undergraduate
       (2) Graduate
       (3) Professional

    I. Enrollment in special programs (These programs could include educationally or economically deprived students, students older than the traditional age group, physically handicapped students, or foreign students.) Institutions, such as community colleges, will have needs that frequently fall in this area.

    J. Residence
       (1) On campus
          (a) Dormitory
          (b) Other
       (2) Off campus
       (3) Commuters (Distance of commuting may need special consideration for personal time in library.)

2. Faculty

    A. Number of faculty by department, program

    B. Number of faculty by academic rank

    C. Number of teaching assistants (graduate students with teaching responsibilities)

3. Staff

    A. Number of staff in teaching-related units (e.g., academic departments)

    B. Number of staff in nonteaching units (e.g., university president's office)

4. Administrators

    A. Number of administrators in teaching-related units (e.g., academic departments)

    B. Number of administrators in nonteaching units (e.g., university president's office)

5. Nonuniversity users (e.g., citizens in community, legislators, high school students, professional and industrial researchers, etc.)

Academic Research Programs

1. Courses taught

    A. By level (100, 200, etc.)

    B. By department

    C. Enrollment in courses

    D. Research programs (e.g., interdepartmental or interdisciplinary activities)

    E. Courses requiring library use for reserve readings, finding suggested readings, and research projects

2. Undergraduate degree requirements

3. Master's degree requirements

4. Doctoral programs

5. Professional programs (law, medicine, library schools, etc.)

6. Special programs (evening school, credit-free programs, etc.)

Much, if not all, of this data may already be available. The institution's research office, or perhaps the central administrative unit, may have compiled the data for accreditation or other reports. Much time will be saved if the information can be obtained outside the library.

To determine the need for library-use instruction, information on users' needs, effectiveness of current programs, and performance levels of students in areas where library use is required is needed. Systematic survey questionnaires, interviews, or other formal methods can be used to gather this information. The type and means of gathering that information should be designed according to the kind of institution for which the program is being developed and its size. Consider the following groups when evaluating users' needs.

Students

If possible, it is helpful to assess the library skills that students have when they enter the institution. This assessment can be done by sampling incoming students with questions that measure basic library skills. It is also helpful to determine the students' attitudes about past library orientation and/or instruction and their perception of the need for instruction in relation to their academic work. In addition, students should be asked their opinions of the library and its resources and about their ability to use these resources.

Pretests measuring existing library skills would be helpful. The student sample should include students in a variety of academic disciplines and at different levels. It would be useful to survey undergraduate and graduate students separately, since the needs and knowledge of the two groups differ. Student responses, especially the attitudinal ones, should be carefully examined.

Faculty

Faculty (including graduate teaching assistants) frequently have needs for library instruction for their own use of the library. Their interest in structuring library instruction in their course work is likely to be enhanced when they are comfortable using the library themselves. Surveys should attempt to identify what personal library instructional needs faculty have. Faculty should also be surveyed to determine the need for library use in their classes, their opinions of students' needs for bibliographic instruction, and their opinions of the types

of bibliographic instruction that would most effectively reach students at each level. Faculty will more likely explore ways to build library instruction into their courses rather than defend present practices if they are encouraged to identify areas of their curriculum which could be enriched by library use.

Academic Administrators

Determine the instructional needs academic administrators have for their own use in the library. Gather administrators' opinions of students' needs for bibliographic instruction and the priorities of library instruction in supporting the curriculum. Their knowledge of available financial resources should prove useful, as well as their willingness to provide other types of resources for a library instruction program.

Institutional Staff

Institutional staff (e.g., academic advisors) might be surveyed to determine their own job-related and individual research needs and their opinions of students' needs for bibliographic instruction.

Outside Users
(e.g., government, business and industry, general public)

Librarians (and other library staff)

Library staff should be surveyed to determine what library instructional needs they may have. Such information is valuable in structuring staff development programs within the library. Librarians and support staff should be surveyed to determine their opinions of students' needs for bibliographic instruction. Frequently, the types of reference questions answered daily by the staff will provide insight into areas where instruction and orientation are needed. Also, data about who is asking the questions will help in identifying groups on which to focus. The library staff might be asked to react to the information gathered in the surveys, especially the student survey. That information will be valuable in involving librarians and library staff in the instructional program.

Many academic libraries have developed instruments which may be adapted for use in other institutions. Samples of various questionnaires, surveys, etc., can be borrowed from the Library Orientation/Instruction Exchange (LOEX) collection. If your library is not currently a LOEX member, consider joining. For a small fee, a vast collection of materials designed by others will become available. If you prefer to design your own instruments, valuable guidance may be found in *Evaluating Bibliographic Instruction*, published by the American College and Research Libraries Division of the American Library Association.

ASSESSMENT OF CURRENT ACTIVITIES

To identify what instruction is needed, it is essential to examine what instructional activities are already in place. In addition, data should be gathered about staff participation, facilities, and equipment currently in use. As a part of this assessment consider:

1. Programs in existence:

    A. Orientation—Are tours of the library currently being given? Is information about policies and services presented?

    B. Course-related instruction—Are librarians or others currently making presentations to specific classes or groups? Do required assignments rely on library instruction?

    C. Credit courses—Is the library or some academic department teaching a library skills or research course? What information is presented?

    D. Point-of-use materials, handouts, study guides—Are printed materials which explain or illustrate use of specific resources used or made available? Are pathfinders or search strategies distributed?

    E. Self-paced workbooks—Are self-teaching materials used in courses or available to individuals who wish to learn more about library searching?

    F. Are library signs a clear and effective aid to independent use of the library?

2. Staff currently participating:

    A. Librarians—How many librarians are already giving tours and class presentations or preparing printed materials? What are their other responsibilities?

    B. Support staff—What clerical or technical staff is assisting these librarians? What are their other responsibilities?

3. Facilities and equipment currently in use:

    A. Facilities—Are classrooms being used for presentations? If not, where are instructional sessions held?

    B. Equipment—What audiovisual equipment is in use? What restrictions does the equipment place on the space used? (E.g., Is a darkened room needed? Does sound disturb study nearby?)

Essentially, before a program is launched, the question to answer is: What library instruction is most needed by the students? The faculty? Other groups on and off campus?

The data gathered from this assessment procedure will generate a profile of instruction needed by the academic community and of the resources available to meet those needs. The profile should also include a history and rationale for the data collection, the data itself, and any commentary needed to help clarify and interpret the data.

Obviously, no new program can or should attempt to meet every instructional need. However, by identifying all the library users needing attention, the library staff can more objectively put their needs in priority order and address the *most* needed area first. Other areas can be added as time, staff, and resources allow.

The profile from this needs assessment will be used to develop the instructional program appropriate to your specific academic institution. Decisions based on this profile will include groups targeted for instruction, goals and objectives for the program, selection of teaching methods, necessary human and financial resources, and initial planning for evaluation of the program.

Searching the Literature

The literature on library instruction is so voluminous that any literature search should focus on specific issues or problems identified in the needs assessment. The target audience, the program's goals and objectives, searching strategies, instructional modes, and evaluation problems are examples of focused issues that might require a literature search for additional ideas or information. The sources in the bibliography of this handbook will help you. Pay special attention to the following:

1. ACRL *Bibliographic Instruction Handbook.* Contains chapters on guidelines, needs assessment, administrative considerations, program timetables, and modes in instruction and evaluation.

2. ACRL *Organizing and Managing a Library Instruction Program, Checklist.* Contains very detailed checklists for elements of a model library instruction program: assessing students' needs, establishing the classroom instructor's interest in bibliographic instruction through an interview, soliciting the dean's interest, administering the program, developing instructional modes and materials, planning inservice programs for training librarians to teach, evaluating the program, gaining and maintaining collegial support within the library, and eliciting institutional support.

3. Conference symposium papers. National conferences have featured some excellent programs, and Pierian Press's *Library Orientation Series* has published several of their proceedings.

4. Major compilations of articles on library instruction. The subject heading "Library Orientation—addresses, essays, lectures" will pick up many of these compilations in your library and on national databases.

5. LOEX. This national clearinghouse for sample materials on library instruction collected by Eastern Michigan University's Center of Educational Resources in Ypsilanti, Michigan, publishes a quarterly newsletter, *LOEX News.* Upon request, LOEX will lend this material for examination. Its conferences also highlight current concerns for library instruction developers.

6. State library instruction clearinghouses. Some state library associations are able to direct you to state clearinghouses for sharing library instruction materials.

7. Indexes and computer databases. The following manual and computer indexes provide access to sources included in the bibliography of this manual. These should be used to identify additional sources, as well as update the list:

   - *ERIC/CIJE*
   - *Education Index*
   - *Library Literature*
   - *LISA*

Consultants

While the use of this handbook and similar guides will facilitate the planning and development of a library-use instruction program, the expertise of others who have developed successful programs can still be useful. Some states have a library instruction section in their state associations that may assist in identifying experts who would be able to offer advice. Many academic institutions have in-house consultants who are able to offer advice on instructional development and simple evaluation. Occasionally academic departments will accept a special project (e.g., program evaluation) for a student practicum under faculty direction, and this energetic kind of help can give library planning welcome impetus.

Sometimes a professional consultant makes sense, and there are guidelines to help determine whether or not to engage a consultant and what the consultant can be expected to do. For example, a professional consultant may be useful if library planners lack confidence in their ability to design and implement an instructional program or to model their program after another institution's program which closely meets the library's objectives.

Choosing a Consultant

Predetermine what should be negotiated up front. Decide whether you want a consultant to guide you, make one or two quick visits to provide assistance, be on a retainer, or preside in the library during the total program development. You will want a written contract to articulate your expectations very clearly.

The consultant must understand what is expected. Determine where planners feel confident to do their own work and where they need help. The more planners execute themselves, of course, the less the services of the consultant will cost. General direction and periodic review from the consultant may be sufficient for most aspects of development, and later in-depth service can be obtained when needed.

In order to adapt an existing program, search the literature to locate proven programs that would meet the library's objectives. Then contact the originating library to determine who developed its program, and interview the person about his or her experience and availability. Review the library's needs to determine what services are expected and for what fee. Interview former clients of the consultant, if any. Ask about services rendered, their evaluations of those services, and their recommendations of the consultant.

What to Expect of a Consultant

The consultant's role can range from an adjunct advisor to the developer of any part or all of one's program. It is best not to have the consultant do all the work. The idea is to learn from a consultant in order to develop in-house skills in planning and management. If the consultant comes on board and does everything, most of that expertise will disappear when the consultant is gone. Since undoubtedly the program will be revised after the pilot phase, it would be well to have some arrangement for continued consultation.

DEVELOPMENT OF PROGRAM GOALS AND INSTRUCTIONAL OBJECTIVES

Selecting the audience should be tied to long-range goals for a library-use instruction program. If the overall goal is to reach 100 percent of the student body at the point where they can best use the instruction, consider the level of instruction required for students as they move through the curriculum (e.g., orientation for freshmen, basic research strategy for sophomores, subject emphasis and advanced strategy for juniors and seniors, tutorial assistance for graduates, etc.). Instruction may have already been developed for some of the areas and any new focus will need to take into account current practice, resources, and personnel available.

Program goals are used to articulate long-range plans for library instruction and to plan phases for development of the program. Information gathered in the initial needs assessment will help to identify areas requiring attention. Program goals state in positive terms plans for satisfying these identified needs. For example, your assessment might identify a need to familiarize students with the current literature resources available in the library. This need would then become the goal: Students will be able to locate significant current information.

Once goals for the program have been written, instructional objectives are written which delineate how the goals will be met. The ACRL Policy and Planning Committee, Bibliographic Instruction Section, suggests that instructional objectives be subdivided into Terminal Objectives and Enabling Objectives (ACRL Handbook, pp. 35-45).

Terminal objectives are the main activities the student will be able to do as a result of your instruction. *Enabling objectives* are implied abilities, that is, those behaviors necessary to achieve the terminal objectives. A terminal objective for selecting the best periodical might read:

> Given a list of topics suitable for a research paper and a list of periodical indexes, the student will be able to select appropriate indexes for finding periodical articles on each subject 100 percent of the time.

This example illustrates three key elements:

1. The *conditions* under which the students will operate and the resources they will have at their disposal (given a list of topics suitable for a research paper and a list of periodical indexes ...).

2. The *behavior* the student should be able to carry out as a result of taking the instruction (... the student will be able to select appropriate indexes for finding periodical articles ...).

3. The *criteria* or standard the student should aim at. This should be attainable but set criteria high. Sometimes 100 percent is desired; sometimes it is not that important. If you want 100 percent say so, whether you reach it or not.

The behavior is *not* defined in terms of what the instructor will teach or what the student will learn. By emphasizing the student's behavior or action rather than the instructor's teaching (the student *will be able to select appropriate indexes*), the focus remains on the assessed needs of the student. The statement in terms of an activity makes it possible to measure actual performance. It is possible to learn a concept and still not be able to perform it, but it is unlikely to perform without understanding.

Terminal objectives, on the other hand, should be formulated for each element of the research process that will be taught:

- *Orientation*—locating key personnel, call numbers, locations of library materials.

- *Basic skills*—key concepts of library catalog usage, periodical indexes, other library indexes.

- *Basic strategies*—organization strategies for using guides to the literature and major works by authorities, etc.

- *Specialized reference sources*—research tools within disciplines, such as bibliographies, catalogs, dictionaries, directories, handbooks, digests and reviews, indexing services, etc.

- *Advanced research*—organizing sophisticated research for advanced courses.

The initial program needs to focus on the most appropriate instruction level based on the abilities and experience of the selected audience. When that is known, terminal objectives can be established to emphasize the learning activities the group needs to achieve.

Enabling objectives identify those behaviors or abilities necessary to perform the terminal objectives. In most cases several enabling objectives are required for the student to successfully perform the terminal objectives. Look at a slightly expanded version of the terminal objective components previously listed:

- *Condition*—Given a list of ten topics suitable for a research paper and a list of six general and scholarly indexes to periodicals.

- *Behavior*—The student will be able to select appropriate indexes for finding articles on each subject.

- *Criteria*—100 percent of the time.

This objective needs several enabling objectives specifying what the student will need to do to perform the expected task. To support the above terminal objective, enabling objectives should be written for the: (1) subject content of each index listed, (2) inter-relationships between the indexes, and (3) practice exercises used to develop the skill of selecting the indexes. An enabling objective for dealing with subject content of indexes might read:

- *Condition*—Given definitions of the contents of *Readers' Guide, Social Science Index, Art Index, Music Index, General Science Index, Applied Science Index,* and a list of these six basic indexes.

- *Behavior*—The student will be able to match each definition with the correct index.

- *Criteria*—100 percent of the time.

Figure 2.1 illustrates the goals, terminal objectives (labeled T), and enabling objectives (labeled E) for an instructional program developed for graduate students at Ohio State University. This model can help you appraise instructional objectives of current programs as well as design objectives for new programs.

There is always a tendency to teach more than the student needs to know. Objectives should be checked further by developing test questions for each objective and administering them as a pretest to the students for whom the instruction is being designed. If students already know the information, that objective should be eliminated from the instruction.

Graduate Students

Bibliographic Instruction

A. Goals

    1. Instructional Goal:

    Graduate students are able to use the library system efficiently and effectively.

    2. Program Goal:

    Through a variety of approaches, graduate students are to receive advanced course-related instruction by the end of their first year.

B. Objectives

    1. Instructional Objectives: (Terminal and Enabling)

        T.a. Students are able to use LCS and the card catalog to find the information they need.

            E.1. Students demonstrate the ability to do all types of searching on LCS and in the card catalog and understand the information on the screen display and catalog cards.

            E.2. Students can identify the correct subject headings for their topics in *LCSH* and apply the information to efficient subject searching in LCS and card catalog.

            E.3. Students demonstrate the ability to use cross references and tracings in LCS and card catalog.

        T.b. Students are familiar with reference sources at the graduate level.

            E.1. Students can identify and locate such general reference sources for researching at the graduate level as *Dissertation Abstracts International, NUC,* OCLC.

            E.2. Students can identify and use the specialized reference sources for their subject area.

        T.c. Students use the search strategy concept in meeting their information needs.

            E.1. Students can develop a complex search strategy in their subject areas.

            E.2. Students can develop an efficient search strategy outside their subject areas.

            E.3. Students can use an efficient search strategy to keep current in their fields.

    2. Program Objectives:

        a) Offer at least one workshop on new and/or special tools such as *SSCL* each quarter.

        b) Increase general and specialized course-related bibliographic instruction by 20 percent each year.

        c) Develop research and subject guides which are uniform in format in each individual library/area reaching 5 or more libraries annually.

        d) Offer broad discipline related Graduate Students Research Strategies Clinic at least three times each quarter (FWS).

        e) Identify research method courses offered and faculty who teach them by fall, 1984.

        f) Contact and work with at least one faculty member who teaches a graduate course by fall, 1984.

        g) Offer at least one new course-related bibliographic instruction session every quarter (FWS).

        h) Develop a credit course in bibliographic instruction using a team-teaching approach with Main Library Reference librarians and subject specialists by 1989.

        i) LCS workshops: Offer at least 5 general workshops each quarter and at least one scheduled LCS lecture in every individual area each quarter (FWS).

C. Present Needs:

    1. Research strategies for each individual area.

    2. MIC information.

    3. List of subject research people.

    4. LCS Brochures.

    5. Transparencies.

D. Future Needs:

Computer program by 1986.

Fig. 2.1. Program goals and objectives from Ohio State University.

It is this crucial stage of program development—when audience and program goals and objectives are determined—that presents the most difficulty for community college librarians. The complications derive from the wide gamut of academic skills, the variety of educational goals, and the resulting uneven patterns of enrollment. The range of academic skills in a single class might include:

- the academically well-prepared student, including the honors student

- the under-prepared or low-achieving student, including those who have dropped out or flunked out of a four-year institution

- the returning adult student who often lacks confidence in his or her academic prowess but is hard-working and typically high achieving

- the non-English-speaking student

Many of these community college students have high expectations but few skills, which cause a high threshold of anxiety and frustration.

Community college students' educational goals differ widely too, and can include any of the following:

- those planning to transfer to four-year institutions

- students picking up a single course or short series of courses to update job skills for promotion or job change

- students seeking a terminal degree or certificate in a technical program

- students seeking to improve their basic skills

- students taking courses for intellectual stimulation or pursuit of a hobby.

Because of these diverse goals, enrollment in community colleges is a mix of full-time and part-time students who are not necessarily enrolled continuously. Job, family, finances, and self-motivation all cause the student to drop in for a while and then drop out for a while. In addition, most community colleges serve a nonresident population with a higher national median age (about 28) and a higher proportion of ethnic and racial minorities than that served by traditional four-year institutions.

Any community college librarian's vision of a well integrated, incremental library instruction program is compromised by this unique, unpredictable community college population. And the key to providing effective library instruction programs to such a diverse student body is to make available equally diverse methods of instruction for all types of learners at every level of research, from the very basic to the advanced.

SELECTION OF INSTRUCTIONAL METHODS

Once the library instructional needs have been identified, the current programs reviewed, an audience targeted, and the program goals and objectives written, the next step in the planning process is to select the instructional methods most suitable for the program.

A common planning error is to make decisions about modes of instruction too soon. For example, the decision to produce a videotape or slide program is made and *then* producers consider the question, "What should the content be?" In order for the instruction method to evolve organically, you must first understand your audience's needs, then your goal, next your content, and finally select what method or mode you will use to present the information.

Figure 1.1 (pages 10-13) shows the seven most common modes of instruction, together with the advantages and disadvantages of each (the pros and cons). A review of this chart will be helpful when you begin to consider which modes will be most effective and practical for your situation.

When selecting the mode of instruction, keep in mind ease of revision. A videotape may be an exciting and professional method of teaching users how to search an online catalog. However, if you wish to add new modules or buy new terminals, your tape will need costly revisions. A slide set or audiotape is easier to update and may be just as effective.

Library Orientation

Library orientation is familiarizing your users with the physical arrangement of the library and its services and policies. If you include this in your list of goals for your program, you have a variety of options from which to choose. Among them are:

- personally guided tours

- audiotaped, self-guided tours

- printed guides

- signs

You may wish to use a combination of modes, which will allow you to reach the widest possible audience.

As you put together the content of your orientation, consult staff to determine what questions about the facility are most commonly asked and which collections are frequently needed. (See figure 2.2 for tour guide information.) Questions which are directional or informational (e.g., Where are the magazines? or What are your hours?) may easily and inexpensively be answered with signs.

A complete introduction to the facility will require a tour, either guided or self-guided. If you opt for personally guided tours, you must determine who will give the tour and when it will be available. Will you require appointments or will drop-in tours be given? Your tour guide need not be a full-time staff member. Students, graduate assistants, or community volunteers can give excellent tours if they are provided an adequate

PENFIELD LIBRARY
Information for Tour Guides

GENERAL INFORMATION	GENERAL LOCATIONS
LIBRARY COLLECTION • Total Volumes, 379,000 • Documents, 184,000 • Microforms, 1,457,000 • A/V material, 55,000 • Current Periodical Subscriptions, 1,950 Total Circulation, 180,000 per year Books are shelved by Library of Congress System - NOT Dewey Decimal System	**BASEMENT** • Special Collections and College Archives
USUAL LIBRARY HOURS (Hours are extended during exam periods, shortened during intersession.) • Mon.-Thu. 8:00 a.m.-11:00 p.m. • Friday 8:00 a.m.-10:00 p.m. • Saturday 11:30 a.m.-10:00 p.m. • Sunday 12:30 p.m.-11:00 p.m. For most current hours, check at Circulation Desk. 24 Hour Room available on main floor.	**FIRST FLOOR** • Circulation/Reserve Desk • TOMUS Terminals • Information Desk • Reference Room • Library Instruction Room • Law Collection • Browsing Collection • Photocopiers • Micro Lab • 24 Hour Room
"Card" Catalog has been replaced by automated catalog known as **TOMUS**. Terminals are available on each floor of the Library. **CIRCULATION/LOAN PERIOD** • Circulating Collection, 1 month • Reference Material, Newspapers, Magazines - LIBRARY USE ONLY	**SECOND FLOOR** • Periodicals/Media Desk • Magazines/Journals/Newspapers • Media Collection • Microfilm Readers • Photocopiers • CMC (Curriculum Materials Center) • Juvenile Collection • Day Carrels • TOMUS Terminals • Government Documents
OTHER SERVICES AVAILABLE • Personalized Reference Assistance • Databases on CD ROMs • Photocopiers • Microfilm Readers and Copiers • Interlibrary Loan	**THIRD FLOOR** • Circulating Book Collection • Circulating Art Print Collection • Study Areas • TOMUS Terminals

Fig. 2.2. Example of guided tour information.

script of information. To create the script, take a walk through the library, noting important collections, areas, and supportive data which should be mentioned. An adequate personally guided tour may be given using notecards containing tour stops and data to include at each stop. Put one stop on each card, and list important facts, policies, and other data to mention at each stop. Number the cards in order of occurrence.

Using this method will ensure that each tour, regardless of who is guiding it, will be similar to the others.

If you opt for self-guided audiotaped tours, be sure to provide a map of the facility, noting appropriate stopping points. The map helps prevent new users from becoming lost along the way and functions as a handout for later reference (see figure 2.3 for a sample of tour map).

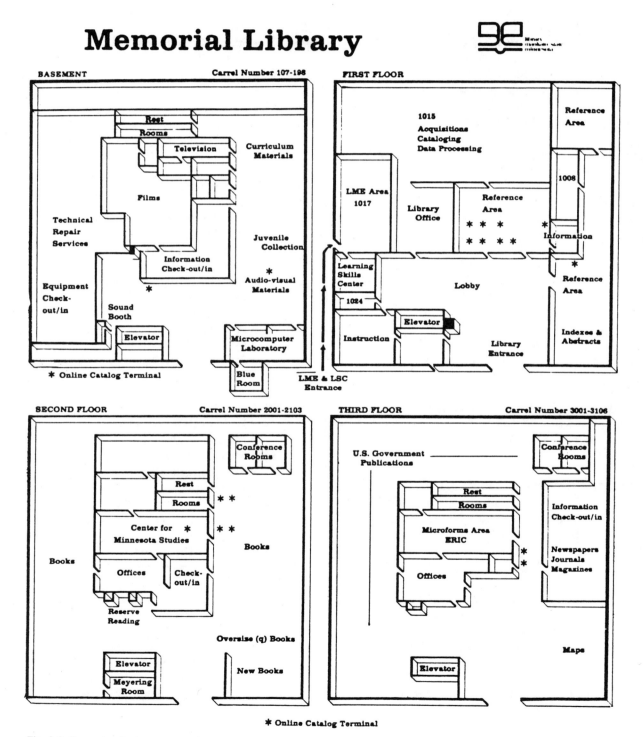

Fig. 2.3. Example of a tour map.

To produce a self-guided tour, you will need to determine the content of the tour, and then write a script containing *every word* which will be spoken on the tape. The final script should also contain parenthetical information, noting appropriate pausing points and the length of each pause. Keep in mind that the voice on the recording is an important consideration. The speaker need not be a professional announcer, but the voice should be pleasant and easy to understand, and the script should be read at a reasonable pace. Even the best script will be unsuccessful if the speaker sounds dull, disinterested, or unclear.

Printed guides can also satisfy library orientation needs and require far fewer personnel. They should contain information on important collections, maps, and library policies and services.

Bibliographic Instruction

Bibliographic instruction (BI) includes activities designed to teach about information resources and research techniques. Keep in mind the pros and cons of each mode (see figure 1.1,

pages 10-13) as you make your selection. As with orientation, your program goals should indicate what instruction is needed, and your instructional objectives will highlight specific topics with which to deal.

When instruction is course-related, discuss library goals and objectives with the course instructors. What do *they* see as the purpose or reason for the library instruction? How is the instruction related to the curriculum for the course? What projects or assignments will the students be expected to produce? The follow-up activities the students complete are crucial to your preparation for the presentation. If the course instructors want the students to have the library instruction "for their own good," or worse yet, because a "babysitter" is needed to free the instructors' time, the students are likely to perceive the library instruction as irrelevant. The more closely the instruction is tied to their actual coursework, the more likely the students are to recognize its value.

(Figure 2.4 is a pathfinder in a game format. Though designed for in-house instruction for librarians, it can be adapted for use with business students and graduates embarking on their first job interviews.)

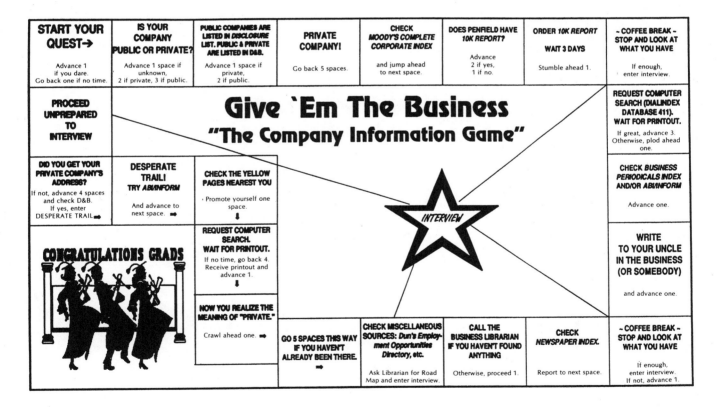

Fig. 2.4. Example of bibliographic instruction game plan for professional staff that can be adapted for course-related classes.

EVALUATION OF
THE PROGRAM

The component of a library instruction program which probably receives the least attention is evaluation. Evaluation is time consuming and can be complicated. In addition, the arena of evaluation can be threatening, especially for a fledgling instruction librarian. For whatever reasons librarians resist evaluation, it is an extremely important component of the program and must be accomplished if a program is to be truly successful.

There are several areas of evaluation which should be considered: student's learning, content of instruction, and method of instruction. Information gained from student exercises or assignments can obviously be used for grading purposes. The same results can also reveal weak areas of student learning, thus identifying additional instruction needed or, if the content is adequate, perhaps the need for a more effective teaching method. Gathering this evaluative data also enables the librarian or the administrator to develop a strong case for continuing support for the instruction program.

Evaluation can take a variety of forms. Formal evaluation can be accomplished through the use of pre/post-tests, questionnaires, surveys, or other forms which gather written comments (see figure 2.5 for sample of pre/post-test, and figures 2.6, page 34, and 2.7, page 35, for samples of student questionnaires). Less formal methods of gathering input include interviewing students and faculty, informally gathering comments and reactions, and observing student performance following instructional sessions.

Evaluation of library instruction activities in the community college setting does not differ much from that done in four-year institutions. However, it is important to note that in community colleges the grading of any library instruction quiz or worksheet should be nonpunitive (e.g., satisfactory/unsatisfactory) since the results reflect the library instruction as well as students' progress. Another consideration in community colleges is the student body's mixture of abilities and experience; one student's understanding of a single concept could be a giant step compared to another student's completion of the entire program.

NAME_____

CAREERS IN CRIMINAL JUSTICE

Library Component
Pre/Post-Test

TRUE-FALSE:
Answer the following using the words TRUE or FALSE. Do NOT use T or F, or any other abbreviations.

_____ 1. The online catalog currently lists all items found in Memorial Library.

_____ 2. Professional journals, rather than books, should be used when the most up-to-date information on a topic is needed.

_____ 3. Other indexes besides social sciences indexes or abstract services will contain information related to the social sciences.

_____ 4. Memorial Library receives all U.S. Government Publications.

_____ 5. The best way to locate U.S. Government Publications is to use the online catalog.

_____ 6. The "call number" for a U.S. Government Publication is called the Superintendent of Documents Number.

_____ 7. If a TERM search in the online catalog yields no matching records, the library has no books on the topic.

_____ 8. Journal articles in Memorial Library cannot be identified using the online catalog.

_____ 9. As compared to using an index, using an abstract service adds an additional step to the research process.

_____ 10. Departments, agencies, and committees can be used as authors in the author section of the Index to U.S. Government Publications.

_____ 11. Getting a "call number" for a U.S. Government Document involves following the same steps as in using a periodical index.

_____ 12. The major difference between an index entry and an abstract is that an abstract summarizes the article in addition to providing the citation.

_____ 13. If a journal article is not available in Memorial Library, the best way to obtain it is to go to another library and look for it yourself.

_____ 14. The "Public Service Serials Title List" includes titles and call numbers for magazines available in Memorial Library.

MATCHING:
Match the MOST APPROPRIATE starting place with each of the following information needs. Answers may be used more than once. Some answers may not be used.

Information needs:

_____ 15. for a reference to publications from the F.B.I.

_____ 16. for a reference to a specific magazine article and a summary of the article

_____ 17. for a reference to a book on crime

_____ 18. for references to articles in *Federal Probation*

_____ 19. for a reference to a newspaper article containing information about crime in major American cities

Starting places:

1. an abstract service

2. an index

3. the online catalog

4. *The Monthly Catalog*

5. *The Index to U.S. Government Periodicals*

6. *The Encyclopedia of Associations*

7. the career information files

Fig. 2.5. Sample of a pre/post-test from Mankato State University.

LIBRARY INSTRUCTION EVALUATION

Please answer the following questions as honestly as possible. Your comments will be used as part of the evaluation of this course and will be considered in the course revisions which are done. Please write on the back if necessary. You are not expected to sign your name, but you may do so if you wish.

1. What class level are you? (circle one)

   Freshman   Sophomore   Junior   Senior   Graduate   Other _____

2. With respect to actually helping you use the library resources and services, how would you rate this course?

   Poor   Average   Useful   Excellent
   1   2   3   4   5   6   7

3. What recommendations do you have for additions/deletions in the content of this course?

4. Did you have difficulty relating lectures to assignments? (Doing after hearing?)

5. Were audiovisual materials used helpful? Why or why not?

6. Which topic(s) was/were especially good?

7. Which topic(s) needed improvement? How would you make these improvements?

8. Was the instructor helpful? Approachable?

What other comments do you wish to make?

Fig. 2.6. Student questionnaire from Mankato State University.

1. Have you taken Library Orientation 101?   (1) Yes   (2) No

2. Is "Careers in Criminal Justice" taken:

    (1) in your major?
    (2) not in major, but required for program?
    (3) an elective?
    (4) other?

3. Your class:

    (1) Freshman   (4) Senior
    (2) Sophomore   (5) Graduate Student
    (3) Junior   (6) Other

4. Did you attend the library session of this course?   (1) Yes   (2) No

DO NOT CONTINUE IF ANSWER TO QUESTION #4 IS NO.

- -

Respond to the following in regard to the library session of this course.

Response scale: X   Not applicable
                   1   Strongly disagree
                   2   Disagree
                   3   No opinion
                   4   Agree
                   5   Strongly agree

5. The librarian's use of visual aids helped me understand the lesson.

6. The librarian explained unfamiliar terms.

7. The librarian's handouts were valuable as learning aids.

8. The library session was worthwhile in terms of obtaining information for this course.

9. Enough class time was devoted to the library lesson.

10. Too much information was included in the library session.

11. The session was worthwhile in terms of obtaining general knowledge of the library.

12. The library session as a whole was valuable to me.

13. Because of the session, I feel more at ease about using the library.

14. The information provided was useful when completing my assignments for this course.

15. The librarian's presentation was interesting.

16. The information provided was useful when completing assignments for other courses.

17. The librarian was well informed on library resources and sources.

18. Because of the session, I am more self-sufficient when using the library.

19. The information provided me was at a level appropriate to the course.

20. The librarian was well prepared for the session.

Fig. 2.7. Another student questionnaire from Mankato State University.

STAFFING

Inevitably, as part of the development process, planners will need to address the question of how the program will be staffed. In a library with a small number of professionals, the instructional responsibilities may be shared by everyone, or one or two may assume primary responsibility for all instruction. However, the larger the staff or talent pool, the more important an organized staffing plan becomes.

Staffing and Personnel

The BI staff should be made up of a variety of individuals including not only librarians, but also support staff and student employees. Frequently, the staff may already be available on campus and it is not necessary to hire new staff to accomplish the necessary tasks. Therefore, it is a good idea to review existing staff before assuming new staff must be added.

Librarians provide the actual instruction, alone or as members of a teaching team. They should be selected on the basis of subject background, teaching experience, technical expertise, and their motivation and commitment to the program. A wide variety of courses and workshops is available for improvement of needed teaching skills. Consultants can also be used to provide local in-service training.

Support staff should be available to assist with the use and production of audiovisuals, instructional use of microcomputers, typing, and marking workbooks or assignments. Student staff can assist with basic clerical tasks, such as typing, filing, and photocopying.

Staffing Patterns

While a variety of staffing patterns is used, three are commonly found: incorporating instruction into the reference unit, creating a separate service unit or department for instruction, and using subject specialists or bibliographers as the instruction staff. There are advantages and disadvantages to each approach.

Incorporating Instruction into the Reference Unit

Probably the most common staffing structure is to assign the responsibility for instruction to the reference unit. A major advantage of this approach is that it increases the overall expertise of the staff involved. Combining the reference desk duties with exposure to users' classroom requirements broadens the librarians' understanding of their clients' needs and, consequently, improves reference service. In addition, the added exposure enhances the librarians' ability to work effectively in collection development, since they see firsthand what may be needed to support the curriculum. A third advantage of this approach is that the reference librarians frequently are in a position to identify areas needing instruction through the patterns of questions at the reference desk.

The major disadvantage of superimposing instructional duties on the reference department is that it increases the work of the reference librarians, who may already be overloaded. This can sometimes create conflicts in individuals' priorities and exhaust the staff. Eventually this overload may cause a morale problem if duties cannot be reassigned or rearranged to lessen the strain.

Creating a Separate Instruction Services Unit

Establishing a separate service unit made up of staff whose primary responsibility is orientation and instruction has three major advantages. First, since the staff have no conflicting duties, instruction can be made available whenever the academic faculty need it, rather than when it fits in around desk duties or other assignments. The instruction staff then has the flexibility to offer the instruction for day classes, evening classes, or even weekends, if need be. This service orientation is especially important when attempting to establish a new program. In addition, the academic faculty never has to feel they are asking for the "favor" of the instruction. It is not an "extra" duty; it is the librarian's "job" to provide the instruction.

A second advantage is that the staff can be carefully selected to provide skills that can meet whatever instruction requirements and opportunities arise. Combining a variety of backgrounds (humanities with science, teaching experience with database expertise, for example) will create a solid, mutually supportive teaching team.

Finally, a separate service unit provides needed visibility for the instruction program. When they are clearly noted on an organizational chart, the instruction librarians take on an instant identity and become a recognizable group within the library staff.

While creating a separate unit has strong advantages from the academic faculty's point of view, there are two drawbacks to this approach from the library's point of view. One is that by setting the instruction staff apart, the library loses the opportunity to tap into their enhanced reference skills. This can be partially offset by including the instruction librarians in the evening or weekend reference rotation. In addition, isolating the instruction staff restricts their regular contact with library patrons at the reference desk and reduces their opportunity to spot needed instruction.

Subject Specialists and Bibliographers

In libraries where the subject specialists or bibliographers have been assigned the responsibility for library instruction, the assumption is that this approach takes advantage of the individual's understanding of the discipline. Undoubtedly, the academic faculty recognizes the research talents of these individuals, and this lessens the faculty's resistance to the librarians doing the teaching. However, if bibliographers have little day-to-day contact with the students, especially undergraduates, they often do not have a realistic understanding of the students' lack of research skills. The end result may be instruction which presents a more comprehensive and sophisticated set of tools and skills than the users are able to cope with.

The Library Instruction Coordinator

Regardless of the method of program staffing selected, planners would be wise to identify or designate one individual as the library instruction coordinator. The coordinator need not be a new staff member. An existing librarian interested in library instruction and familiar with the local situation would be a good choice. The coordinator serves as the focal point between the staff and other campus groups, acting as go-between when necessary. The single contact person facilitates referral of instruction requests and identifies the appropriate librarian for the needed instruction. The coordinator should have the authority to oversee all instruction offered, thus insuring consistency of the program. In addition, the coordinator should have the authority and knowledge to provide for staff training when needed.

BUDGET

Budget as it is used here refers to one-time and continued financial support of the library instruction program and includes equipment, materials, travel, and facilities, as well as personnel, which has previously been discussed.

Equipment

The equipment needed is that which best supports the instructional objectives. Be careful not to select the medium or mode of instruction and equipment first and then force the objectives to fit. Select equipment according to the results of the needs assessments, goals, instructional objectives, and budget available for the program. Some equipment will require a library expenditure; some could be borrowed from a central equipment pool on campus in many cases. In community college libraries which function as a part of a learning resources center, easy access to the audiovisual unit's instructional equipment may obviate the need to purchase additional equipment for library instruction.

Equipment which may be needed includes:

- Microcomputers, in the library as a preexisting lab, as a special purchase for library instruction, or elsewhere on campus.

- Portable terminal and/or CD-ROM equipment, to be used for instruction in database search demonstrations in classrooms.

- Electro home projector, a device which transmits the image from a microcomputer onto a screen for classroom instruction.

- Videotape equipment, including a camera and playback equipment—useful for evaluation of teachers and creating video programs.

- Slide/tape equipment, including 35mm camera, flood lights, projector, and recording equipment.

- Overhead projector, one of the most used pieces of equipment in library instruction, and a portable, wired cart.

- Cable TV equipment and studio (not documented in the literature, but not outside the realm of possibility).

- File cabinets (a much needed item which seems to be the hardest thing to acquire).

- Typewriter or word processor (constant revisions make the latter almost essential).

- Sign equipment—everything from stencils to a kantograph; many signs can be done most easily on a microcomputer with appropriate software.

- Photocopies—mundane but essential; not mundane if sophisticated enlarging, two-sided copying, etc., are available.

Ongoing Expenses

Most of the equipment you have or will need requires supplies of some sort or another, such as:

- Software programming languages like BASIC or PILOT or commercially developed programs, PLATO (Williams and Davis, 1979; Eng, 1984).

- Videotapes, either those which are commercially produced, borrowed from LOEX, or locally produced using library resources, university public relations staff, campus educational media staff, or alumni who happen to be local TV celebrities (Jacobson, 1983).

- Videotapes, those which are used exclusively to evaluate library instruction.

- Film and blank tapes, for slide/tape presentations done in-house.

- Transparencies produced on campus in the library using a thermofax or photocopy machine, or in the educational media department—also nonpermanent transparency markers.

- Stock for signs.

- Workbooks—many academic libraries are using variations of the UCLA model (Renford, 1978; Phipps, 1979; Wood, 1984).

- Classroom handouts, whether self-developed or LOEX adaptations (will need periodic review and reprinting).

- Database searching performed in the classroom to demonstrate its use as a way of preparing students to perform their own preliminary research (Dreifus, 1982; Markiewicz, 1984), or to teach students to do their own database searching (Ward, 1985). An educational password can be obtained to allow searching in DIALOG, Wilsearch, or Search Helper at reduced rates, and evolving CD-ROM products can be used to reach ever wider audiences.

Travel Funds

Many college and university libraries have line items in their budgets for faculty/staff development, but library instruction added to other staff travel needs makes the pie just that much smaller. Travel to LOEX conferences or Earlham College workshops, as well as ALA conferences, is often very helpful for library instruction coordinators and other staff, even if budgets cannot promote frequent attendance.

Facilities

The major one-time expense to consider is facilities. One can use classrooms outside the library and have walking tours—guided or self-guided—through the library, or use the whole library as a classroom. However, when the library can be renovated to accommodate a new library instruction program, the plans and expense should be carefully considered (Farber, 1984).

Options to consider are:

- Providing additional office space for library instruction personnel as a place to confer with students or to prepare materials.

- Providing storage for equipment, sufficient quantities of printed materials, files of original instructional materials, etc.

- Constructing a suitably large classroom—one or more—near the entrance to the library or near the reference room, complete with blackboard, projection screen, adjustable lighting, multiple outlets in strategic places, and a dedicated telephone line for online search demonstrations.

- Converting part of the reference room to a classroom by either ·partitioning or rearranging furniture and shelving.

- Arranging the entire library in order to reinforce library search strategy (Earlham College). (See figure 2.8 for a sample facilities assessment form.)

Determining budget requirements is only part of the picture in planning a new library instruction program. Finding the money or in-kind services to meet these needs is the name of the game. Some suggestions for funding:

- National grants for large or innovative programs.

- Local college or university grants for the development of new programs or for junior faculty.

- Vice president for academic affairs, provost, etc. (The University of Alabama gets $30,000 a year for graduate teaching assistants from this source. Keever, 1976)

- Departments for whom library instruction is most important, such as the English department (Wiggins, 1985).

- Large campuses may have an educational media department which does graphics, photography, audio- and videotaping for classroom instruction.

- Campus public relations offices may have staff artists, photographers, etc., to share.

- Testing and evaluation departments on campus.

- Line item in the library budget.

- A "piece of the pie" from the existing library budget categories, such as equipment, postage, personnel, travel.

- Some of the expenses can be passed on to students by selling items such as workbooks through the bookstore for a profit (Pennsylvania State University), or through the department which uses them, such as external degree or independent study.

SPACE/ROOM _____ Library Instruction Area _____ Total net square feet __1,300__

STRUCTURE [Note Number]		**PURPOSES/FUNCTIONS:** To provide space for library instruction for twenty students using a variety of audiovisual equipment. Also provide for some individual self-paced learning. Work area for staff.
walls	[1]	
windows	[ ]	
doors	[ ]	
floors	[ ]	
ceilings	[ ]	
other	[ ]	

UTILITIES

		ACTIVITIES: Lectures and group discussions. Students do lessons and take tests. Four individual learning stations. Preparation of instructional materials including graphics. Storage of AV instructional materials, hardware and software.
electrical	[2]	
plumbing	[ ]	
mechanical	[ ]	
other	[ ]	

ENVIRONMENTAL

		SPECIAL CONSIDERATIONS: Maximum security area. Work counter should be provided with a sink if possible. AV storage area and a projection booth can be combined.
thermal	[3]	
acoustical	[4]	
visual	[5]	
esthetics	[ ]	
other	[ ]	

MEDIA SYSTEMS

		SPATIAL RELATIONSHIPS: Adjacent to and direct access to Library reading room. Group activities in instructional area should not interfere with the individual learning stations.
audio	[ ]	
tv	[ ]	
CAI	[6]	
AV	[ ]	
other	[ ]	

NOTES:

1. Area must be enclosed by floor to ceiling wall; work area and instructional area can have an office partition.

2. Must have sufficient electrical outlets placed in front and rear of instructional area.

3. Films and slides require 60°-70° temperature.

4. Must provide soundproofing so noise does not spill over into Library reading room.

5. Lighting should have a dimming switch.

6. Contain power requirement for 3 microcomputer stations.

FURNITURE AND EQUIPMENT: Twenty chairs with writing tablets; instructor tabledesk and chair; chalkboard; projection screen and speakers; workcounter with storage for supplies and equipment for preparing instructional materials; storage closet for AV hardware and software; 4 wet carrels for microcomputers and individualized learning.

Fig. 2.8. Sample facilities assessment form.

PUBLIC RELATIONS

Public relations refers in the end to the impressions others have of the library, of the library instruction program you are hoping to promote, and of you as a professional with a unique set of qualifications.

Publicity for Programming

When starting a library instruction program, you will go through the steps which have been suggested earlier: deciding on the target group through needs assessment, developing the program, publicizing that program, presenting the program, and evaluating what you have accomplished. The important activity at this point is the publicity. The program will fall flat if the audience you wish to attract does not show up. Some suggestions on how to reach people on a campus include:

Library staff:

- announcements and discussions at meetings

- newsletters, brochures, flyers, posters, displays

- one-to-one discussion

Faculty (all faculty, new faculty, those who already use your services for library instruction):

- announcements or presentations at faculty meetings (campus-wide or departmental)

- sending personal letters, via campus mail or in the form of electronic mail

- one-to-one in the library or in the faculty member's office

- one-to-one at social gatherings (in library, on campus, at church, in your home, etc.)

- through their students

- items in faculty/staff newsletter

- enclosure in new faculty packet which your college or university sends out

- general mailing of request forms

- library open house with refreshments

Students:

- posters, signs, and displays in the library or student union

- through faculty members

- handouts in library, at the student union, or at registration

- student newspaper articles (This method is rather risky since the students decide what they want to print and may opt against what they consider to be dull library stories. To be sure of inclusion, buy an ad.)

- one-to-one discussions

- announcements to panhellenic organization

- library open house with refreshments (See figure 2.9 for sample publicity flier; figures 2.10 and 2.11, pages 42 and 43, for sample posters.)

Self-Promotion

Establishing credibility for you and the library instruction program takes visibility and rapport with the teaching faculty. Ways to attain this include:

- Advanced degrees in subject disciplines help promote collegiality.

- Professional association membership and involvement should be made known to the teaching faculty.

- Talk about your research interests with faculty and have citations for your publications listed in the annual college or university faculty publications list.

- Be sure your annual report for library instruction or a brochure on the program gets channeled to appropriate persons—those who fund the program (Brundin, 1985).

- Be informed about faculty research interests and help them keep current by sending copies of tables of contents of journals and subject lists of new acquisitions; provide document delivery if possible.

- Develop a library instruction program for faculty (Johnson, 1984) or graduate assistants.

- Provide a mechanism for criticism, such as a suggestion box or "bitch tickets" (University of Connecticut); this also works as a vehicle for praise. Answers to complaints are often instructive and should be publicized.

- Participate in some campus and community activities, such as faculty senate, university-wide committees or task forces, faculty interest groups (AAUW, AAUP), university social groups (university women's club, faculty club), university or community choral groups (oratorio society, community chorus), amateur theater group, university-associated church, Friends of the Public Library volunteer or board member, PTA membership, athletic groups (campus recreation center, jogging events, student academic advisor, sorority/fraternity advisor, and community service organizations (Optimists Club, Jaycees, etc.).

GET INTO THE SWIM OF COLLEGE LIFE

TAKE

LIBRARY ORIENTATION

LME 101

Learn how to use —

ON-LINE CATALOG
INDEXES + ABSTRACTS
MICROFORMS
GOVERNMENT DOCUMENTS
MUCH, MUCH MORE

General Education elective
One Credit

DON'T MISS THE BOAT

TAKE

LIBRARY ORIENTATION

LME 101

Learn to use —

ON-LINE CATALOG
INDEXES + ABSTRACTS
MICROFORMS
GOVERNMENT DOCUMENTS
MUCH, MUCH MORE

GENERAL EDUCATION ELECTIVE   ONE CREDIT

Fig. 2.9. Sample publicity flier from Mankato State University.

Fig. 2.10. Sample poster from Mankato State University.

Graduate Student Research Workshops

A SERIES OF WORKSHOPS DESIGNED FOR GRADUATE STUDENTS BEGINNING MAJOR LIBRARY RESEARCH.

Each presentation will include:

Planning Your Research

HOW TO CHOOSE A TOPIC AND DETERMINE APPROPRIATE SOURCES FOR YOUR TERM PAPER, THESIS OR DISSERTATION.

Computerized Searching

HOW TO UTILIZE LCS (THE LIBRARIES' COMPUTERIZED CATALOG) AND ONLINE COMPUTER SEARCH SERVICES OF THE OSU LIBRARIES.

Sample Subject Search

A DEMONSTRATION VIA LARGE-SCREEN PROJECTION OF LCS AND ONLINE COMPUTER DATABASE SEARCHING.

ALL WORKSHOPS WILL BE HELD IN ROOM 120,

BAKER SYSTEMS ENGINEERING

5:00 - 7:00 P.M.

- TUESDAY, APRIL 23 - RESEARCH IN THE ARTS & HUMANITIES
- WEDNESDAY, APRIL 24 - RESEARCH IN THE SOCIAL SCIENCES
- THURSDAY, APRIL 25 - RESEARCH IN THE SCIENCES

Fig. 2.11. Sample poster from Ohio State University.

PROGRAM SUPPORT

A successful instructional program needs staffing, training of instructional staff, budget, physical facilities equipment, and supplies. To obtain these, the support of campus and library administrators, colleagues, and academic faculty will be needed. Take time in the early stages of planning to assess the needs and to review all steps of a program with appropriate personnel. Surveys indicate that most institutions do not begin with enough personnel for a full-blown library instruction program. For this reason, it is advisable to begin with realistic goals and to build the program gradually as additional support is gained.

Academic support is invaluable. If the desire is to work with academic departments, it is helpful to identify faculty members who consistently assign library work to their students and who themselves are regular users of the library. These members of the faculty are more likely to cooperate in developing an instruction program, and this basic networking can be instrumental in the initial selection of the audience.

This procedure is effective at every level of the curriculum. By selecting an audience where there is academic support and by promoting library instruction as enrichment for an existing curriculum, the library can gain strong allies in different departments. One of these academic departments may be willing to cooperate to begin a pilot program for specific courses. After the program has proven itself, a department may even consider contributing to it financially. Another cooperative venture is team teaching a segment of a course. The involvement of librarians and faculty in course or class design can improve course offerings and strengthen collegial support for the library's vantage.

In the community college setting, the primary focus is on teaching rather than on research. In these settings, the faculty tends be open to ways of improving instruction and hence are perhaps more responsive than the average college or university faculty member to working with librarians to improve student library skills. It is also true that the community college has a greater proportion of part-time lecturers than most four-year institutions; and while they are often very receptive to library use instruction, lecturers are frequently difficult to reach and to keep notified of new resources and services.

It is important to realize that securing faculty support is ultimately tied to the soundness of program development. A quality program will sell itself. Proven results can be proudly communicated to library and campus administrators; a report documenting improved performance by students as a result of the instruction will generate interest in the program. Keep this interest alive. Extend personal invitations to colleagues and administrators to see firsthand what the library is doing. Programs can fail to receive support if decision makers have false impressions because they never see the program firsthand. This happens too frequently when programs are developed from the grass roots and communication lines are not kept open regularly. Program support requires program promotion.

By following this procedure, the growth of the instruction program will frequently take care of itself. Academic faculty whose students benefit will broadcast a collegial respect that is contagious, and administrators will be eager to encourage its expansion if at all possible. This increased support can later be used to build into the budget the necessary personnel, physical facilities, and equipment and supplies. With this kind of foundation, the prognosis for a permanent and healthy instruction program is good.

GETTING STARTED: SUMMING IT UP

The number of considerations involved in planning a library instruction program may seem overwhelming. Preliminary planners should deal with the following questions, with more details filled in later as program plans become more fully developed:

- What instruction is needed?
- What priority should be given to each need?
- Which needs will be dealt with first?
- What instruction (if any) is currently available? (Include tours, printed materials, class presentations, self-instructional materials, signs.)
- Who is doing the instruction?
- What staff support is currently in use?
- What are the goals of the program?
- What priority should be given to each goal?
- What objectives will help meet those goals?
- What modes of instruction may be used to attain each goal?
- Should different modes be used to support varying objectives?
- Would a combination of modes be appropriate?
- How will the program be evaluated?
- What instruments will be used?
- Will new instruments be designed or will existing instruments be adopted?
- How will the program be staffed?
- What organizational method will be used?
- How will the program be financed?
- Will additional funding be necessary, or will the program be "taken out of hide"?
- What facilities and equipment will be needed?
- Is enough classroom space available? If not, where will presentation be given?
- How will the program be publicized?
- What advertising will be needed?
- How will you gain faculty and administrative support?

Preliminary answers to these questions create the basic outline for the academic library instruction program. Later, the sketchy plan will flesh out as the program gets under way. Considering all aspects early in the planning process will help ensure a well-organized effort and a good measure of success.

SELECTED BIBLIOGRAPHY

Articles

Brundin, Robert E. "Help Your Administration Support Bibliographic Instruction." *Reference Librarian* 12 (Spring/Summer 1985): 129-34.

Cipolla, Katherine. "M.I.T.'s Point-of-Use Concept: A Five-Year Update." *The Journal of Academic Librarianship* 5, no. 6 (1980): 326-28.

Cottam, Keith M. "Conceptual Planning Method for Developing Bibliographic Instruction Programs." *The Journal of Academic Librarianship* 7 (September 1981): 223-28.

Dreifuss, Richard A. "Library Instruction in the Database Searching Context." *RQ* 21 (Spring 1982): 233-38.

Eng, Sidney. "CAT and the Future of Bibliographic Instruction." *Catholic Library World* (May/June 1984): 441-44.

Engeldinger, Eugene A., and Barbara R. Stevens. "Library Instruction within the Curriculum." *College & Research Library News* (December 1984): 593-98.

Farber, Evan Ira. "BI and Library Instruction: Some Observations." *Reference Librarian* 10 (Spring/Summer 1984): 5-13.

Fields, Carolyn B. "Using Results of a Pre-test to Determine Lecture Content: A Case Study (of Health-professions Majors at San Jose State University)." *Research Strategies* 5 (Winter 1987): 29-35.

Forrest, C., and M. Gassmann. "Development of a Self-Guided, Audiocassette Tour at a Large Academic Library: Preliminary Report." *Research Strategies* 4 (Summer 1986): 116-24.

Hofman, Lucinda A. "Educate the Educator: A Possible Solution to an Academic Librarian's Dilemma." *The Journal of Academic Librarianship* 7, no. 3 (1981): 161-63.

Jacobson, Gertrude N., and Michael J. Albright. "Motivation Via Videotape: Key to Undergraduate Library Instruction in the Research Library." *The Journal of Academic Librarianship* 9, no. 5 (1983): 270-75.

Keever, Ellen H., and James C. Raymond. "Integrated Library Instruction on the University Campus: Experiment at the University of Alabama." *The Journal of Academic Librarianship* 2 (September 1976): 185-87.

McLaughlin, P. "Teaching Methods for Bibliographic Instruction: A Selected ERIC Bibliography Prepared for ACRL Continuing Education Course 202." *Information Reports and Bibliographies* 14, no. 5 (1985): 3-4.

Markiewicz, James, and Linda Guyotte Stewart. "Quicksearch: Computer Searching for Undergraduates at Cornell University." *The Journal of Academic Librarianship* 10 (July 1984): 134-36.

"Model Statement of Objectives for Academic Bibliographic Instruction: Draft Revision (of the 1979 Model Statement)." *College & Research Libraries News* (May 1987): 256-61.

Pastine, Maureen. "Library Instruction and Reference: Administration of a Bibliographic Instruction Program in the Academic Library." *Reference Librarian* 10 (Spring/Summer 1984): 181-89.

Phipps, Shelley, and Ruth Dickstein. "The Library Skills Program at the University of Arizona: Testing, Evaluation, and Critique." *The Journal of Academic Librarianship* 5 (September 1979): 205-14.

"President's Program" on "Raising Funds for Libraries: Paths to the Private Sector." Presented at the ALA President's Program, Chicago, 1984.

Reich, P. "Choosing a Topic in a Research Methods-Oriented Library Instruction Program." *Research Strategies* 4 (Fall 1986): 185-87.

Renford, Beverly L. "A Self-Paced Workbook Program for Beginning College Students." *The Journal of Academic Librarianship* 4 (September 1978): 200-203.

Roberts, Maureen. "How to Generate User Interest in Library Orientation and Instruction: Some Practical Suggestions." *Bookmark* 38 (Fall 1979): 228-30.

Ward, Sandra N. "Course-integrated DIALOG Instruction." *Research Strategies* 3 (Spring 1985): 52-64.

Wiggins, Marvin E., and Elizabeth Wahlquist. "Independent Library Usage: A Research Strategy." *The Journal of Academic Librarianship* 11 (November 1985): 293-96.

Williams, Mitsuko, and Elisabeth B. Davis. "Evaluation of PLATO Library Instructional Lessons." *The Journal of Academic Librarianship* 5 (March 1979): 14-19.

Wood, Richard. "Impact of a Library Research Course on Students at Slippery Rock University." *The Journal of Academic Librarianship* 10 (November 1984): 278-84.

Books

Adams, Mignon S., and Jacquelyn M. Morris. *Teaching Library Skills for Academic Credit*. Phoenix, Ariz.: Oryx Press, 1985.

Association of College & Research Libraries. Policy and Planning Committee, Bibliographic Instruction Section. *Bibliographic Instruction Handbook*. Chicago: Association of College & Research Libraries, American Library Association, 1979.

Association of College & Research Libraries. Bibliographic Instruction Section Continuing Education Committee. *Organizing and Managing a Library Instruction Program, Checklist*. Chicago: Association of College & Research Libraries, 1979.

Beaubien, Anne K., Sharon A. Hogan, and Mary W. George. *Learning the Library: Concepts and Methods for Effective Bibliographic Instruction*. New York: R. R. Bowker Company, 1982.

Breivik, Patricia Senn. *Planning the Library Instruction Program*. Chicago: American Library Association, 1982.

Clark, A. S., and K. F. Jones. *Teaching Librarians to Teach: On-the-Job Training for Bibliographic Instruction Librarians*. Metuchen, N.J.: Scarecrow Press, 1986.

Mager, Robert F. *Preparing Instructional Objectives*. Palo Alto, Calif.: Fearon Publishers, 1962.

Mellon, Connie. *Bibliographic Instruction: The Second Generation*. Littleton, Colo.: Libraries Unlimited, Inc., 1987.

Oberman, Cerise, and Katina Strauch. *Theories of Bibliographies Education: Designs for Teaching*. New York: R. R. Bowker Company, 1982.

Renford, Beverly, and Linnea Hendrickson. *Bibliographic Instruction: A Handbook*. New York: Neal-Schuman Publishers, Inc., 1980.

Vargas, Julie S. *Writing Worthwhile Behavioral Objectives*. New York: Harper, 1972.

PART III
PUBLIC LIBRARIES

Planning an Instruction Program in a Public Library

Kathleen G. Woods
Municipal Information Library
Minneapolis Public Library
Minneapolis, Minnesota

Helen T. Burns
Elsie Quirk Public Library
Englewood, Florida

Marilyn Barr
Ritner Children's Branch
The Free Library of Philadelphia
Philadelphia, Pennsylvania

INTRODUCTION

A public library is an expression of the community it serves. The reading levels, employment levels, ethnic groups, languages, age levels, lifestyles, and educational resources are some of the qualities that define a community and determine the mission of its public library. These same qualities determine the kinds of instructional programs that are needed by a community.

Library instruction in some form has been one of the services provided by public libraries as long as there have been open stacks; however, the instruction offered in public libraries is often informal and ad hoc. Usually it is given as part of the reference transaction. By instituting a formal program of instruction, a public library is not so much introducing instruction as a function of the library as it is formalizing this function. This formalization helps public libraries maintain the quality, appropriate content, and consistency of instructional offerings they may already have in place. With the guidance of this handbook, it also helps each library determine the special needs of its community and develop a customized program of instruction that will meet those needs.

NEEDS ASSESSMENT

The Library and the Community

The library's mission and its role in the community are defined by the library board's and the library staff's perception of who the community is and what the community's needs for information are. If the library is to serve its community's needs, if the library is to embody an expression of its community's culture, the library must have as much information as possible about that community. It is hard to overstate the importance of the fundamental steps of community needs analysis in all library planning. As communities differ so do the roles, missions, and activities of public libraries. In order for a library to best meet its public's current and projected needs, these needs must first be determined. This can be done by gathering and analyzing information about the community.

Various aspects of the community should be analyzed, such as demographics, occupations, lifestyles, etc. Before collecting any data, carefully determine what questions need to be answered, the extent of community information already gathered, the quantity and type of data needed, and available resources. The ability of staff to collect and interpret data should also be assessed at this time, since gathering of data is considerably easier than interpreting it. Raw data is seldom informative but must be transformed into percentages, comparisons, or projections. Plan to get an outside consultant's help if needed, or locate a resource person in another municipal office.

The following is a list of data needed and possible sources, plus steps for conducting surveys. Gather data from a number of years, so you can spot trends and shifts.

1. Analysis of population in the geographic area to be served

    A. Age (total, children, teenage, early adult, etc.) Be sure to match age categories with library's age-related definitions.

    B. Sex

    C. Family life cycle (young singles, married with children, etc.)

    D. Income

    E. Occupation

    F. Education levels

    G. Race and nationality

    H. Languages spoken

    Information available from:

    Census data

    City planning office

    Government reports

    Zoning office

2. Library Utilization

   A. Who uses the library? Categorize all possible user groups.

   B. Who does not use the library?

   C. What is the library used for? How is it used?

   D. Barriers to use — geographical, physical, psychological. Pay particular attention to the comments of nonusers.

      Information available from:

      Community and user surveys

      Interviews with community leaders, staff, and representatives from community organizations.

3. Transportation situation

   A. Which segments of the community use a car? Public transportation?

   B. How long does it take to get to the library?

      Information available from:

      Marketing studies

      City planning office

      Newspaper reports

      Transportation headquarters

4. Business

   A. Typical businesses and employers in community

   B. When and where do consumers shop?

   C. Is there a particular day, season, or hour associated with activities?

      Information available from:

      Telephone yellow pages

      Local directories

      Newspapers

      Planning office

      Chamber of commerce

5. Organizations (cultural, educational, recreational)

   A. How do people spend their leisure time?

   B. What organizations do people belong to?

   C. What are the dominant organization(s) in the community?

   D. Is there a particular time/season associated with participation?

      Information available from:

      Surveys

      Interviews

      Chamber of commerce

      Planning office

Guidelines for surveys:

1. Preparing the instrument

   A. If you are unfamiliar with preparing and conducting surveys, seriously consider using a resource person or consultant.

   B. Decide what information should be gained from the survey.

      (1) Users' and nonusers' perceptions regarding access

      (2) Frequency of visits

      (3) Purpose of visits

      (4) Knowledge of library resources and services

      (5) Satisfaction with library resources and services used

      (6) Utilization of other information resources in the community

   C. Examine other library surveys to see if their questions can be used or adapted.

   D. Consider from whom you want the information.

   E. Check reading level. Is it appropriate for the entire target audience?

   F. Keep the survey short to encourage participation.

   G. *Always* pretest the survey with a small group similar to the target audience to check for errors and misunderstandings.

2. Conducting the survey

   A. Reaching the target audience.

      (1) Going door to door or telephone surveying is most successful.

      (2) Using the mail or the local newspaper is the least successful.

   B. Samples need to be large enough to be representative of the target group.

C. When surveying users in the library, sample at different times and on different days of the week to get representative results.

D. Consider how the survey will be evaluated.

E. Consider the library's personnel skills and resources for surveying. What training and preparation are needed?

THE NEED FOR INSTRUCTION

Let's assume that the foundation, consisting of a current community profile and a set of library goals based on the community profile, is in place. Planning for a library instruction program begins here: (1) Who is the community you serve? (2) What are their needs? (3) What are the library's goals?

Some instructional needs will come directly from the community profile. For example, if immigrants move into the community, their cultural, educational, and language needs will affect the instruction program. Another example is changing age patterns of the population; an increase in young children or an influx of retired persons will change instructional needs. Members of the library's public often suggest ideas for possible instruction quite directly. Keeping a written record of these requests over several months helps to document community needs.

Library staff are in a prime position to observe the need for patron education. Depending on staff size, this can be relatively simple or complex. Librarians and support staff should all participate in brainstorming about possible audiences for instruction. When a group has been identified as a potential audience for instruction, compile a thorough description of the group, its library use patterns, and its instructional needs. This information can be gleaned from some of the following sources: (1) community profile, (2) staff observations, (3) interviews with selected patrons, (4) data from a patron focus group, and (5) a survey of patrons.

A detailed description of the Denver Public Library's internal needs assessment phase conducted in 1985 is included in appendix A to this chapter. Read this through for a thorough, concrete example of methods used to glean information and specific results.

More target groups and more instructional needs within those groups may be identified than is possible to address with the limited resources available for current instructional programs. In this case, target groups and their respective instructional needs must be judged in relation to one another and the planning process continued for those groups and needs that have the highest priority. This ranking is both a practical and a political decision; the goal is to make the most positive, productive impact possible on the community with the library's available resources.

The library's institutional goals and objectives can be important tools for ranking the target groups and the identified instruction needs, especially if annual planning is part of the procedures. For instance, the library's long-range plan might include the following goal and objective.

- Institutional goal: To improve public awareness of the library's information resources and services.

- Institutional objective: To improve access to the main reference library in fiscal year (FY) 1990 for teenagers.

If this goal and objective have a high priority in the library's FY 1990 long-range plan, then instructional programs to improve teenage access to the main reference library would have a high priority in the overall instructional plan for FY 1989.

Probably before the needs assessment—and certainly after—the library administration will need to be involved in the vital role of planning support for the instruction program. Staff time, a materials budget, and facilities should be easier to justify if the proposed program is backed by a careful needs assessment and aligned with the library's overall mission and goals. Interest in the plan generated at this time affects the whole process of designing and implementing the program, so efforts to get administrative commitment is time well spent.

At the conclusion of the needs-assessment process, you will have identified and described the instructional needs of various patron groups that are served by your library. You will have ranked the groups and their needs based on the library's current instructional goals and the political realities within which the instruction program must be developed. With this information, and with the library administration's blessing, you are ready to decide the nature of the instructional program(s) to be developed.

PROGRAM GOALS AND OBJECTIVES

Goals are broad statements of purpose that place the program in the context of the library system's goals and the community's needs. Program goals should reflect the instruction needs of a particular group of patrons and be measurable. The Norfolk Public Library course, called "Using Public Library Resources," has the following goal statement which is geared to a general adult audience:

> Even though each citizen has a "right" to information, we realize that in our present age of technology and computers it is becoming more complicated and difficult for many people to exercise this right by locating the information they need. One of the purposes of a public library is to ensure that books and other library materials which serve informational, educational, and recreational needs will be available to all. The rationale for this course, therefore, is to provide instruction in the competent use of the resources of a public library.

Program objectives are more detailed statements of what will be accomplished by the program. One or more program objectives should be written for each program goal. The following objectives were developed for the Norfolk Public Library's course:

1. To introduce current practices and trends to participants in the use of library catalogs, reference materials, periodical indexes, audiovisual materials, specialized collections (juvenile, government documents, Virginiana, etc.) by a combination of lecture, discussion, and hands-on instructional methods.

2. To provide participants with a basic understanding of bibliographic descriptions, classification systems (both Dewey and Library of Congress) and subject headings which they will encounter in libraries.

3. To improve participants' skills in not only locating what they need in the catalog and within the library, but also in trouble-shooting techniques when problems arise.

4. To guide participants in gaining a concept of the library's place within the community.

Remember that program objectives are not the same as instructional objectives, which are discussed on page 54. Instructional objectives are behavioral objectives that describe learner outcomes resulting from each instructional session. Program objectives are management objectives that describe what will be accomplished by a proposed project.

The program's objectives are derived directly from the goal of the program and, if not ongoing, they should be given a time frame. Either the objective or the action plan derived from the objective should indicate expected performance and means of measurement.

As a general rule, examine the objectives at six-month intervals for progress toward their completion. If an objective has been met, then consider whether it is an ongoing concern that should continue to be part of the library instruction objectives. Also decide whether the objectives have helped you reach your goal in the manner in which you had planned. If an objective has not been completed, check if progress to date is on time frame or content.

For each program objective, write strategies which itemize the separate actions that will be taken to accomplish the objective. These strategies together constitute the action plan. At this point many decisions will be made, such as how many instructional sessions will be needed, what level of curriculum is appropriate (see p. 54), what methods of instruction might be effective (see pp. 52-54), who will prepare/purchase instructional materials, who will make the presentations, where will the instruction occur, what forms of evaluation are appropriate (see pp. 52-53), etc. The strategies clarify specific activities and assign completion dates. They also designate personnel to accomplish each strategy and specify any budget, training, or resources required to complete the activity.

To follow through on a previous example, consider an instruction program for teenagers. Remember the example of an institutional objective cited earlier was to improve access to the main reference library in FY 1990 for teenagers. The following goal and objectives might be adopted for this program.

- Program goal: The aim of this program is to assist teenagers in becoming independent users of the main reference library while enhancing cooperation between the library and the public school system.

- Program objective 1: The program will acquaint teenagers with the resources and services of the main reference library that are particularly suitable for school research projects.

- Program objective 2: The program will be compatible with the needs and desires of high school and junior high school teachers and students.

- Program objective 3: The program will emphasize the ways the public library can assist with research activities outside of school, such as job hunting, bicycle and car repair, travel plans, music, etc.

The action plan for this set of objectives might look like this:

1. Meet with local high school and junior high school teachers and survey a group of students to determine exactly what content should be covered by the program. Who will do this? When?

2. Write a detailed proposal for the program, including instructional objectives, recommended teaching methods and materials, proposed budget, plan for evaluation, etc. Who will do this? When?

3. Prepare the presentation materials and evaluation instruments for each session. Who will do this? When?

4. Arrange for and make the pilot presentation and obtain evaluations. Who will do this? When?

5. Write evaluation report making recommendations for revisions. Who will do this? When?

This action plan identifies tasks that must be accomplished if the objectives are to be achieved and assigns responsibilities. Since plans to evaluate the program are based on program objectives, now is the time to set up the scheme for evaluation.

PROGRAM EVALUATION

Program evaluation is the process of collecting and analyzing information to determine how adequate and effective a program is and to plan future program development. Logically, an evaluation plan derives directly from a program's stated objectives: Does the program achieve the results that its planners set out to accomplish?

A plan for evaluation should be developed at the same time that the program objectives are written. Each objective should have an evaluation strategy that answers the following questions:

1. What do you need to know to determine that this objective has been accomplished?

   Kinds of data that might be collected include:
   - Rates of participation
   - Levels of audience satisfaction
   - Changes in the library skills of participants
   - Observed changes in patron behavior
   - Effective management of the program
   - Changes in attitudes of participants
   - Relation of the program to the needs and interests of the audience
   - Skills of the presenters
   - Effectiveness of separate components of the program
   - Librarian satisfaction with the program
   - Completion rates

2. Who is the audience and what is the purpose of the evaluation? For example, whether the audience for the evaluation is an external funding source or library-based colleagues may affect the selection of evaluation methods.

3. What method(s) of evaluation will provide the information in a form that will meet the needs of the identified audience of the final report? For example, an external funding source may require a series of objective tests that document the achievement of instructional objectives, perhaps a pre- and post-test. On the other hand, if a program is developed by a public library primarily as a public relations effort, documented attendance and participant satisfaction could be the focus of the evaluation.

   Possible methods of evaluation include:
   - Documented rates of attendance; number completing the program
   - Attitude surveys of participants, after or before and after the program
   - Colleague's critique of content, presentation skills, etc.
   - Tests, quizzes, and products, such as bibliographies or assignments
   - Interviews with individuals or groups
   - Comparison of participant and nonparticipant groups
   - Comparison of pretests and post-tests
   - Report of observations of patrons using point-of-use instructional materials

Let us follow once more our example of a user-instruction program for teenagers. One objective that was adopted is:

- Program Objective 1: The program will acquaint teenagers with the resources and services of the main reference library that are particularly suitable for school research projects.

1. How can we know whether this objective has been accomplished? Possible methods of evaluation include:

   A. Rate of participation in the program and the number of teenagers completing it.

   B. Evaluations of program content by teachers, librarians, and teenagers.

   C. Tests or assignments that demonstrate that participants know how to access the resources and services covered in the program.

   D. Changes in the number of teenagers using the main reference library, whether for reference help, study, or circulation of materials.

2. How will the program evaluation be reported? Data and a written report will go to:

   A. Appropriate teachers and young adult librarians.

   B. Library administration, including library board.

   C. Appropriate school administrators.

How detailed a program evaluation needs to be depends on the intended outcomes of the program. If the purpose of the program is largely to enhance public relations with the community, then attendance and participant satisfaction may be sufficient indications of effectiveness. If a program has specific educational aims, then an assignment or test that demonstrates participants' skills is a most appropriate evaluation tool.

Appendix B shows two kinds of evaluation instruments. The Fairfax Public Library form is a descriptive program evaluation which is filled out by the librarian presenting the program. It serves to document: (1) that a presentation took place, (2) where, when, and by whom a presentation was made, (3) who attended, (4) the approximate cost to the library, and (5) a short, informal, evaluation by the presenter.

The Norfolk Public Library asks the participants in its course, called "Using Public Library Resources," to rate how well or poorly the instructional objectives for each session were achieved and to evaluate other aspects of each session such as presentation quality and the usefulness of instructional materials. Appendix B contains the evaluation survey for the third session of this course. Note that this is not the only form of instructional evaluation used in the Norfolk course. Appendix C shows the course assignment that must be completed by participants in order to fulfill the requirements of the course.

The research assignment requires participants to demonstrate that they have had a hands-on experience using the materials, concepts, and skills presented in the classes.

LEVELS OF CURRICULUM AND METHODS OF INSTRUCTION

Public librarians tend to categorize patron use of the library into four common patterns. J. D. Webb describes the patterns this way:

> ... the four user types are: (1) the browser or reader, (2) the researcher, (3) the independent learner, and (4) the group participant. With the exception of the last, the user types form a hierarchy. Each is characterized by a progressively deeper involvement with the professional staff and the technical resources of the collection. Furthermore, the needs of each hierarchical type build upon those of the more initial levels.[1]

These four types of library users are recognized by many librarians. The browser wants to use the library casually, in a hit or miss fashion, with as little interaction with the professional staff as possible. The researcher is looking for the answer to a specific question and becomes involved with professional staff and library tools and services to the extent necessary to answer that question. The independent learner's aim involves more extensive research with a longer time commitment, and it usually engages the library staff and services more than the other use patterns.

Interestingly, library instruction programs have traditionally addressed these same types of library users. Three distinct kinds of library instruction have evolved and they coincide with the needs of the three user patterns identified by Webb. Library instruction is commonly categorized as: (1) orientation, (2) instruction in the use of library tools, or (3) instruction in the research process.

Orientation is an explanation of the floor plan of the building, the physical arrangements of the collection, the hours and policies relevant to public service, and other general information about the library, the library system, and local library and information networks. This level of instruction is designed so that the browser will be able to use the library comfortably.

Instruction in the use of a specific research tool, such as a periodical index or online catalog, consists of a detailed and practical explanation of how to use that tool. It is called point-of-use instruction when the transaction takes place at the time and in the place that the patron is ready to use the research tool. This focused type of teaching is often useful to the researcher who needs to find the answer to a particular question.

As noted earlier, the user patterns identified by Webb form a hierarchy of progressive involvement with the services and staff of the public library and, likewise, these levels of instruction build upon each other in the complexity and depth of their exploration of research skills. The third level of library instruction, teaching the process of research within a body of literature, aims to teach both the bibliographic structure of a body of literature and the decision-making process that is followed in a search within that literature. This kind of instruction is especially useful to the independent learner.

It may be helpful to identify which of these user patterns would benefit most by instruction and then develop a program for that type of user. Of course, an instruction program can address more than one of these levels of research skills, but the desired results and teaching methods should be explored fully in the planning stages. Probably the most common mistake made in bibliographic instruction is to develop a program that consists of one or two presentations, usually lectures, which present a hodge podge of information that includes bits and pieces of orientation, particular tool explanations, and research process skills all mixed together. This kind of presentation almost invariably overwhelms and confuses the patron.

For information on the various teaching methods and how to choose appropriate modes see "Selecting Teaching Methods" (pp. 10-13) in the "General Overview." Public library instruction often relies on methods that allow the most flexible scheduling, for example, printed materials, signage, and point-of-use explanations. Since public libraries must meet the needs of the widest range of users, patrons' language and reading skills are a prime consideration. In some environments, simple graphics on signs and multilanguage audio and written guides will be essential.

INSTRUCTIONAL CONTENT AND MATERIALS

The instructional content of a program is derived from the program objectives. In order to detail exactly what must be covered to fulfill the requirements of the program objective(s), those objectives must be translated into a list of instructional or learning objectives. Instructional objectives state what a library patron will be able to do as a result of participation in the instructional program. These objectives are sometimes called learning outcomes and they should be stated in measurable terms whenever possible.

A simple procedure that facilitates deriving instructional objectives from program objectives is to write each program objective that relates to instruction on a separate sheet of paper. Then, on each sheet, list all the things that program participants must know or be able to do if that objective is to be achieved. Write instructional objectives from the point of view of the learner and explicitly state what the participant will be able to do as a result of the program.

Once again, follow the example of an orientation program for teenagers where the first program objective is:

- The orientation program will acquaint teenagers with the resources and services of the main reference library that are particularly suitable for school research projects.

The instructional objectives itemize what participants will need to know in order to have a working knowledge of the resources and service of the main reference library, for example:

- Where the main reference library is and how to get there.

- The floor plan of the main reference library.

- Services available at the information desk and at reference desks.

- Hours of the library.

- Circulation and use policies.

- Special collections and service.

- Relationship of the main reference library to other libraries in the system and in the area.

- How to obtain additional information and assistance.

When the list of elements to be covered in the instructional program is complete, the elements are rewritten as separate instructional objectives. Some of the instructional objectives for our orientation program are:

- Instructional objective: Students will know the location of the main reference library and two ways to get there by bus and subway.

- Instructional objective: Students will be able to correctly label the location of the three departments and one special collection on a floor plan of the main reference library.

- Instructional objective: Students will be able to list three services available at the information desk.

The purpose of writing instructional objectives is to explicitly list the content of the instruction in terms that state learning outcomes or the desired results of instruction. When the expected instructional achievements of the program are listed, appropriate methods of instruction can be selected based on: (1) the instructional objectives, (2) the needs and abilities of the target audience, (3) the talents and preferences of the librarians involved, and (4) the budget, time, space, and materials available.

For a more comprehensive discussion of how to write instructional objectives, see part II of this handbook. See appendix C to this chapter for a course outline showing instructional content and a research assignment used by the Norfolk Public Library in its course, "Using Public Library Resources." The assignment requires the participant to follow one subject through many different kinds of information sources. A participant evaluation form used at the end of the third session of the course is part of appendix B. It lists the instructional objectives for that session.

PROGRAM MANAGEMENT

Staff and Budget

Few public libraries hire staff specifically for instruction activities. Current staff usually take responsibilities for the program(s) and make the necessary adjustments in their schedules. If volunteers are used, staff time is needed for recruiting, training, and supervising them. The library director's and trustees' support obtained during the needs assessment stage of planning is essential for seeing the program through nitty gritty decisions at this point. And, communication is a key ingredient in gathering and maintaining ongoing staff support for successful instructional programs. Arrangements must be made to reserve and prepare the space that will be used for instruction. Equipment needed must be reserved and prepared or, perhaps, purchased. There are other program costs to identify and budget: supplies, printing costs, advertising budget, etc. People whose work will be affected by the program should be informed about plans for the program. This includes the circulation desk staff, supervisors, reference desk staff, pages, guards, maintenance, etc.

Publicity and Public Relations

Effective publicity is measured by the degree to which the targeted audience receives, comprehends, and acts upon that message. Publicity is more than the printed word or radio message, however; it includes, but is not limited to, the ambiance of the library, the staff attitudes towards patrons, and the appearance of the library building and surroundings. "A library enjoys good relations with its public as a result of excellent service and use of its materials, not as a result of public relations per se. Fine service means an attention to what urges the public to enter the premises and enjoy the visit."[2] An outstanding instructional program can be adversely affected by these other factors and, conversely, a library with its services in good running order is primed for a positive response to new ventures into library instruction.

The intended audience and the content of the particular library instruction program determines the type and amount of publicity used. As a rule of thumb, one type of promotion method is not sufficient. A program for local businesses might be promoted by mailing flyers to business people and organizations, for example, as well as advertising in the business section of the local paper and announcing the program at business club meetings. Different procedures would be followed, of course, if a very limited audience is desirable.

For the beginner, the most difficult aspects of publicity are allotting adequate time for preparing publicity, contacting people, distributing flyers, generating mailings, and speaking at community meetings. The next hardest task is determining which kinds of publicity are most effective in your community.

1. Guidelines for public library publicity

    A. Who is the targeted audience?

        (1) Age, reading level, language used, physical mobility, etc.

        (2) Characteristics that affect the type of publicity, for example, reads large print, organizational member, etc.

    B. What publicity methods are available?

        (1) How long does it take to produce?

        (2) Does it need to be developed or is it already available?

        (3) How much does it cost? What is your budget?

        (4) Is there adequate time to use this method? Example: the local business organization has a newsletter but it will be delivered the day after your program.

    C. What type of publicity would be most appropriate to reach the targeted audience, for example, radio, newspaper, flyers, etc?

2. Selected types of publicity

    A. Newspaper publicity.

        (1) What newspapers are available?
             (a) Local, daily, church, institution newsletters, etc.
             (b) Which ones will accept press releases and/or articles from the library?
             (c) Name of contact person, deadlines for receiving press releases, and time of publication.

        (2) Format for press releases. (See pp. 71-72 for examples.)
             (a) Always type, double-spaced, on 8-½" by 11" paper.
             (b) Send the newspaper the original and keep at least one copy for your files.
             (c) Use letterhead paper.
             (d) Always include location of program, day of week, date, time, length, cost, and appropriate age level of audience.
             (e) Include release data. Generally, put *for immediate release.*
             (f) Remember to include name, address, phone number, and organizational affiliation for a contact person.
             (g) Put important information first.
             (h) Use regular capitalization.
             (i) Use only one side of the paper.
             (j) *Always* have another person read your press release prior to mailing to ensure accuracy and clarity.

    B. Flyers (See appendix D for examples.)

        (1) How many do you need? When do you need them? Have you allowed sufficient time for distribution? Will flyers be produced in time for distribution at appropriate meetings?

        (2) What language style to use? What languages? What reading level?

        (3) Format
             (a) How long will it take to produce?
             (b) Include location of program, day of week, date, time, length, cost, procedures for preregistration, and appropriate age-level audience.
             (c) Keep text brief, but interesting and informative. Indicate the audience for whom the program is geared.
             (d) *Always* have another person read the flyer copy to ensure clarity and accuracy before it goes to press.

        (4) How and where will the flyers be distributed?
             (a) Internal — at circulation desk, as posters, to other departments or branches.
             (b) External — mailing lists, local agencies, community centers, schools, agency meetings, etc.

    C. Radio public announcements

        (1) Make it shorter than a newspaper release — no more than three-fourths page double-spaced.

        (2) Type all radio news releases on letterhead paper. Send the original. Keep at least one copy.

        (3) Double-space or triple-space copy with wide margins to make it easier for the announcer to read "cold."

        (4) Send it early. Specify release date and time. Include appropriate information on the library contact person.

        (5) Be informal, conversational. Use simple, short, descriptive words and sentences.

        (6) Avoid involved sentences and tongue twisters. Spell out difficult names and places phonetically and put them in parentheses beside the real spelling.

        (7) Don't put your key information first — the initial words are primarily for catching the attention of the listeners.

        (8) Repeat the same thing in different words at least twice.

(9) The rule of thumb for translating words into seconds is:

10 seconds = 25 words

15 seconds = 37 words

20 seconds = 50 words

30 seconds = 75 words

60 seconds = 150 words

(10) Read the script out loud. Does it read well?

D. Community contacts

(1) Be sure to inform key people in the community, that is, the information networkers who can influence people's attitudes and actions.

(2) Be sure all staff members are aware of the program and are able to give out accurate information to public inquiries.

(3) Keep presentations at community meetings brief, interesting, and appealing. The best combination is a short, clear announcement coupled with written handouts on the program.

COOPERATION WITH COMMUNITY ORGANIZATIONS

Requests for public library instructional programs commonly come from the library administration, from desperate program chairs of other organizations, or from librarians observing patrons' needs. Involvement with local agencies can enhance interinstitutional cooperation and promote library resources and services to nonusers. Because of the diversity of outside requests, it is vital that the librarian realistically consider the relation of each request to the library's goals, current staffing, available resources (time, materials, costs), and staff skills and attitudes. Be sensitive to colleagues who may not feel the same enthusiasm for this activity and may resent outreach instruction from the library that may shortchange the staff.

In order to develop an effective program in cooperation with another organization, it is essential to accurately assess the needs and resources of the cooperating organization. The primary obstacle to successful assessment is communication, that is, gaining sufficient accurate information to assess the needed components of this library instruction program. Good communication takes time and cannot be rushed.

What follows is a practical, detailed look at the questions that must be considered:

Checklist for Cooperative Programs

1. Content of program:

A. What topic and style of program is desired by the contact person?

(1) Orientation, lecture, group discussion, instruction in the use of a particular tool or access to a body of literature?

B. How realistic are the goals of the contact person?

C. Do you have a name and address of a contact person?

D. What are the library's goals?

E. What type of program is already available or adaptable? Will this request mean the development of a new program?

F. Intended audience.

(1) Who will actually be there? Entire families? Children? Retirees?

(2) How many?

G. Level of presentation.

(1) Overview, introduction?

(2) In-depth and detailed?

H. Is it feasible? Is there sufficient staff, time, etc.?

(1) What must be prepared?
(a) Script, handouts, etc.

(2) Is sufficient time allowed to present the program?

(3) Can appropriate materials be taken to the program?

I. Where will the program take place?

(1) Is the assigned site suitable, for example, size, acoustics, outlets, etc.?

(2) Is the site accessible to handicapped users?

(3) Can you view the room prior to the library's overall goals?

2. Administrative concerns:

A. Does the program relate to the library's overall goals?

B. Is staff available and capable of presenting the desired program?

C. Is this a good opportunity to send a new librarian with an experienced staff member for training?

D. Is the audience being charged a fee to attend the program?

E. What resources, staff, time, materials, and other resources are entailed?

3. Preparing for the program:

A. Clear program with supervisor and place on schedule.

B. Write confirming letter repeating data in step 1. Give a carbon copy to the supervisor and staff involved; keep at least one copy.

C. Plan what needs to be done by what date; allow for unforeseen emergencies.

(1) Is a program available; must one be developed, adapted?

(2) What handouts or other materials are needed? How many?

(3) Need to book equipment or transportation?

(4) What staff will be involved? Is training needed?

(5) Any pilot testing or rehearsal needed?

D. Identify changes in behavior, attitudes, or skill expected in the audience.

E. Plan evaluation of the program.

4. Be familiar with the equipment:

A. If equipment is provided, is it compatible (e.g., will your slide tray fit on their machine) and is it easy to use? Who will bring it to the program and see to it that it works?

B. If the library provides equipment, be sure it works and has spare bulbs. Take extension cord and adapter and loud speaker, if necessary.

C. Have an alternative plan in case the equipment is not there or does not work.

5. Reconfirm the program with the contact person several days before the date set and reconfirm *everything*. The group may have changed the date, time, place, etc., of the meeting. Go step-by-step through what you expect to do and what you expect to happen.

6. Use effective communication:

A. Show enthusiasm for the topic.

B. Use a clear, pleasant sounding voice that can be heard; enunciate carefully.

C. Make eye contact.

D. Know the material.

E. Gear the program to the needs and interests of the audience.

7. After the program:

A. Evaluate it. How could it have been improved?

B. Return the equipment and materials.

C. Prepare a written report and share it with the library administration.

D. File copies of your materials and notes for future use.

LIBRARY INSTRUCTION FOR CHILDREN: A SAMPLE PROGRAM

Library instruction for children helps to provide the foundation for lifelong learning skills. Whatever children pick up about libraries and resources, formally or informally, continues to evolve and affect their attitudes towards libraries and their information gathering skills. School and public libraries are natural allies in the effort to capture children's innate curiosity and develop these skills. Curriculum-related instruction is the bailiwick of school libraries; public libraries encompass curriculum related instruction, leisure interests, and problem-solving skills.

The key ingredient in children's library instruction is the librarian. Strong interactive skills, a wealth of knowledge about resources for various age levels, creative ability, and a commitment to services all come into play in this role. A children's instruction program needs to spark and sustain their interest if librarians are going to promote library skills that engender independent exploration and learning.

Library instruction for children differs from instruction for adults in that a greater concern must be paid to the child's educational maturation and the school curriculum sequencing. For instance, the parent or the day-care worker, not the child, is the focus of library instruction for children under five years. Library instruction for first and second graders focuses on appreciation and care of materials, awareness of fiction and nonfiction, and identification of parts of books. Orientation to the library, introduction to specific library tools, and the research process all start in the third grade.

Individualized instruction, reinforcement, and realistic assessment of material to be absorbed have a marked importance in children's library instruction. A child's age and attention have a direct impact upon the type of instructional program, the time allotted, and the methods used. Scheduling is a special consideration too, and should occur during quiet times in the library to ensure that the librarian can greet the children and remain with them during their entire library experience. With children's high energy levels and short attention spans, the contact person from the group should remain to assist in providing a positive library learning experience and, later, should provide reinforcement and follow-up experiences for the group. This will greatly aid in the achievement of objectives.

Sample Program for Grades 4-6

This is an experimental program for children in grades 4-6. It is designed to be part of a summer reading program, which is for grades 4-8 and runs for eight weeks during the summer. It is expected that twenty to thirty children will attend each session and that the summer reading program will permit follow-up activities.

1. Planning the program

   A. Needs assessment

      (1) Observe children's knowledge and skill in using the children's room.

      (2) Examine bibliographies of school research papers to determine types of materials consulted and how they are used.

      (3) Compare observed skills, knowledge, and attitudes with those desired by library and local school curriculums.

   B. Purpose and goals

      (1) To improve the ability of children in grades 4-6 in the 1990 summer reading program to do research at any library.

      (2) To assist children in locating sources of information on topics of their choice.

      (3) To increase the children's awareness and use of standard research tools for elementary school students.

      (4) To foster a positive attitude toward the library services and the library staff.

   C. First program

      (1) General orientation—children will be able to locate reference, fiction, nonfiction, game, magazine, and video sections of the library.

      (2) Identification of bibliographic items.

      (3) Catalog instruction—children will be able to search the catalog in two ways and identify call numbers.

      (4) Practical applications.

   D. Second program

      (1) Introduction to reference resources—children will be able to find an encyclopedia article and a book or video on topics of their choice.

   E. Third program

      (1) Practical application of knowledge, for example, scavenger hunt for information.

   F. Evaluation

      (1) Develop pretest and post-test, possibly a pre- and post-scavenger hunt.

      (2) Considerations:
         (a) Were the program goals met?
         (b) Were as many children reached as planned?
         (c) Was the program worth the effort expended?
         (d) Was the desired grade level reached?
         (e) How did participants respond to program?

SUMMARY AND CONCLUSION

A public library's instruction program goals derive from analysis and integration of three arenas: the needs of the community, the institutional goals of the library, and the current political realities within which the library and the community function. From the general program goals, more specific statements of the program objectives are formed. An evaluation method is then developed to match each program objective. For each program objective and evaluation plan, an action plan is laid out, specifying strategies to accomplish them. Each strategy should include a person responsible for accomplishing the activity and a completion date. At this stage, many decisions must be made before the plan can move forward, such as instruction content, instructional objectives, methods and materials, evaluation instruments, administration of the program, coordination with outside agencies, and publicity for the program.

It is important to remember that there is no one ideal instruction program and that it is difficult to make comparisons between libraries because of unique local circumstances. Through creative, careful planning and experimentation, you can devise a program that best suits your local needs. Use this handbook to help you systematically analyze your library public's instructional needs and develop a solid and successful program that reaches into your community. The results will reflect the library's commitment and professional expertise; good planning can only improve government/library/citizen relations.

NOTES

1.   J. D. Webb, "A Hierarchy of Public Library User Types," *Library Journal* (September 15, 1986), 47-50.

2.   Patricia F. Beilke, "Library Instruction in Public Libraries: A Dream Deferred, A Goal to Actualize," *Reference Librarian* 10 (Spring/Summer 1984), 1.

APPENDIX A: EXAMPLE OF A NEEDS ASSESSMENT BASED ON OBSERVATIONS

DENVER PUBLIC LIBRARY
Needs Assessment Report
August 1985
Lynn Roberts, Training Officer

Introduction

Patron education in library use was identified as a high priority by the central management staff. In response to their request for assistance, the training officer conducted a needs assessment to determine specific areas of patron education needs in the central library. The first phase of the assessment, presented in this report, is based upon information gathered in departmental focus groups. Staff knowledge of patrons needs is based upon daily experience in serving a wide range of users. The second phase will be information from groups identified as users of specific collections of the library. This information will provide the database for central managers to set priorities and monitor the use of the central facility.

Methodology

Market research focus groups were held in each central department serving the public by the training officer in June and July 1985. Forty-one staff participated in one-hour meetings designed to determine patron needs from a public service viewpoint. Questions staff answered were:

1.   What basic knowledge and skills would you like patrons to have about how to use the library?

2.   How should we deliver this information? Methods of delivery of information and skills?

3.   What possible market segments can you identify for phase II?

4.   What information needs do you think patrons would pay for? What price would you suggest?

Summary of Staff Focus Groups:

- Patron education needs.
- Possible formats for meeting needs.
- Market segments for phase II.

Patron Education Needs

From the perceptions of staff, the following categories of patron education needs developed:

- User-friendly setting.
- Catalog access.
- Knowledge of indexes.
- Knowledge of reference sources available.
- Knowledge of services available.
- Machine usage.

User-Friendly Setting. Many staff on the first floor say that some patrons act confused, hesitant, and intimidated upon entering the front door. People seem to feel foolish when they have stood in line to ask where bathrooms are located, how to find the children's collection, inter-library loan (ILL), the film center, or a copy machine. In spite of the large letters *information desk*, people will frequently turn to their right upon entering and ask the security guard for assistance, the volunteer in the new books area, or go to the circulation desk for help. Staff throughout the building believe the lobby entrance area of Denver Public Library (DPL) could be much more hospitable and user friendly.

Hand in hand with the need for a less intimidating entrance area is the need for clear directions and locations of the various departments, the equipment available to the public, restrooms, stairs, and library materials. Patrons frequently ask staff what floor they are on, what department they are in, how to get to ILL, the film center, or the children's area. While staff are accustomed to answering such questions, their time on the desk could be more productively used doing reference work. Most patrons would prefer being more self-sufficient in such matters.

The next level of need for clear location is for patrons to know where to find indexes, catalogs, periodicals, and other library materials. Locations of reference books, art prints, tax forms, encyclopedias are not obvious. Many patrons do not know the visible stacks are backed up by two floors of books in sub-basement plus storage at the library annex. Current obscure locational information being visible means that what many patrons think is if they don't see it, it doesn't exist.

Catalog Access. Catalog access during DPL's transition from a card catalog to one that is online has been difficult at best. Patrons need to know that periodicals, documents, films, Western history materials, and paperbacks are not on CARL. In understanding how to use CARL, it is important to know what "available" means and what is not on CARL. Location codes such as BEST, FIE, and SOC are only explained in the *new* section of CARL, and that title is misleading. Serials information that is available on FAXON is not readily available to the public. Since older materials that have not been converted can only be located in the old card catalog on the first floor, many patrons are often sent back "downstairs" (where downstairs?) to start their search over. When this trip is from the third floor, and the patron may have trouble even finding the stairs to the third floor to start with, they are often angry and frustrated when they do discover the Information Desk. To then have to return to the third floor with the correct call number does not engender an image of professional friendly library service.

Knowledge of Indexes. Patrons need assistance in locating and using indexes. The *Readers' Guide*, the *Periodical Index*, and guides on how to buy books such as ABPR and CBI have information helpful to patrons. Staff uses time to instruct or else finds the information for them. Many libraries with short staff cannot give such one-to-one instruction, and some type of self-directed learning aids would be equally beneficial to staff and patron.

Knowledge of Reference Sources. Each department has reference materials that need some explanation or education for the patron in their use. In the past, this has been the area often taught in classes for patrons. However, the class covered all reference sources in the building regardless of the patron's specific interest or purpose. Phase II market segment research on patron's needs may well help target what information resources can be packaged into a class or learning aids. Some aids can be general. Some can be specific for particular patron interests.

Knowledge of Services Available. Many patrons do not know of the extent of services at the DPL. Basic service of a librarian to do reference is not well known to the casual library user. Circulation is the one area that most patrons understand. The value of materials, resources, expertise, and how to access them is not commonly known. Examples of services about which patrons have limited awareness include SURGE classes, placing reserves and where to pick up the materials, what is required to get a library card, how to use the electronic library, DIALOG, duplication capabilities, accessing books outside DPL, how to make recommendations to buy materials, picture files, and the Western history photographs collection.

Machine Usage. Many patrons are aware that DPL offers machines for patrons to use such as copiers, typewriters, and microfiche readers. They do not know where they are located or how to use them. They expect staff to have expertise to fix machines, load paper, and change ribbons. They do not understand when staff is less than eager to assist in these areas. Patrons do not separate providing machines and helping use machines into two separate services—one which the library provides and one which it does not.

CARL PAC terminals do not readily indicate the services they provide. Patrons who are not familiar with PAC will either have to be shown how to use them or will ask for assistance from staff at a desk. Many CARL libraries provide signs giving instructions on usage.

Possible Formats for Meeting Needs

Formats for providing information and skills relating to improving library skill and usage fall into two major categories:

- Self-directed learning formats.
- Staff-directed learning formats.

Self-Directed Learning Formats. Signs, color-coding, maps, printed materials, learning aids, computer-aided instruction, audiotapes, videotapes, broadcasting, cablecasting, newspaper articles—all of these are ways which could meet patrons' needs without involving interaction with a staff member. Staff suggestions as to how to meet the identified need cover a wide range of self-directed learning methods. The following list indicates possibilities which would need to be developed if chosen as the preferred format. Many needs could be met in a variety of ways and a combination of formats may be necessary to cover the different learning styles of patrons.

Need—User-Friendly Setting

- More effective signs.
- Printed maps of the building listing locations of topics such as Dewey locations of stacks.
- Footprints or lines to follow on floor to specific locations.
- Large numbers and colors for what floor you are on.
- Large signs for stairs from second to third and fourth floors.
- Signs such as "Do you need to know?" followed by "Look Here."
- Signs on how to get a library card; what is accepted and what isn't.
- Directories of our services and products and locations.
- Redesign the kiosk to hold instructional materials.
- Self-guided tour on audiotape and walkman.
- Computer-aided instruction on floor description of information and service locations. This could be a menu driven CRT that has what codes mean, where to find, Dewey locations, maps, topics, resources, and services.

Need—Catalog Access

- Signs for CARL PAC—what it is, how to use, what to find, and what to look for elsewhere.
- Sign for what codes mean that they find on PAC.
- Printed information about PAC—limits and what other catalogs exist in building and where (pathfinders might help).

- Where periodicals are located and how to find out information on FAXON. Where to find hard copy and material available on fiche could be printed on a fact sheet handout.

- Where to find films, art prints, tax forms, and videos could be explained on CARL, or via printed materials.

- Information about how to use online searching services to locate materials could be available via video, printed handout, or booklet.

Need—Knowledge of Indexes

- Printed instructions for each index might be developed, or at least indexes could be listed and department locations where they are to be found would be helpful.

- Indexes could be part of a menu-driven, computer-aided instruction package, with locations and purposes they meet.

- A video instruction tape could have a librarian discussing where to find indexes and their purposes.

Need—Knowledge of Reference Sources Available

- There needs to be a listing of what reference sources are available and where. This could be by subject or department. Kate Hager has a prototype design for one.

- A video instruction tape could discuss references and include both the services of the librarian as well as materials.

Need—Knowledge of Services Available

- Video programs could feature services on each floor, department, and subject area. Could be on an audio-tape that combines location as well as services. Could be listed on a directory that is in the stairwells.

- Flyers on each service could be printed.

- Slide tape show could provide the same information.

- Basic video on "How to use the library" that tells where to begin, more than meets the eye, reference materials, storage, ILL, and why you leave books on the table.

- Many "How to ..." videos were suggested on all kinds of specific topics. Almost any class that would be taught in department could be taped and edited for future showing.

Need—Machine Usage

- Self-directed learning on machines would include instructions written near or on the machine, a booklet attached to the machine, or diagrams. Whom to ask for assistance would also be helpful information. Copiers, CARL, micromax, fiche readers and printers, typewriters, and public computers all need to be clearly labeled as to use and function.

Staff-Directed Learning Formats.

Need—User-Friendly Setting

Many staff suggested a floor walker or person who would greet patrons entering the building who seem to be unfamiliar with the setting. Suggestions included training volunteers to do this, using volunteers who are retired librarians, or using a designated staff person. This person could direct patrons to a point where they could pick up self-directed learning materials or to the proper desk to receive more help in person. Tours of the building on a regular basis led by volunteers or trained reference staff (TRS) could provide an additional setting for learning to occur in a more personalized manner.

Need—Catalog Access

Along with tours, generic classes on DPL catalog locations, purposes, and how to utilize could be done on a regular basis by the TRS staff, catalog access to materials for special information needs could be built into almost any specific class offered by a department. Access to shelf-list information could be made available in departments to patrons.

Need—Knowledge of Indexes

Classes in departments could teach use of indexes at both specific and generalized levels. Pathfinders and instruction guides would be useful aids in learning.

Need—Knowledge of Reference Sources Available

Classes would include reference materials on specific subjects that fit the market segment along with the skills to use the catalog, indexes, and online searching for citations. Handouts could either fit the market segment or be more general to use in a variety of classes.

Need—Knowledge of Services Available

Radio talk shows, television shows, and cablecasting could all feature specific services the library provides to help particular groups meet their information needs. Target a wide variety of their needs. Classes could be offered in departments on a regular basis.

Market Segments

The best way to develop ideas that have strong market potential will be through focus groups. Jim Everett suggested bringing in target groups, giving them a questionnaire as to their knowledge of skills on library usage in their area of interest, teaching a class developed by the staff, and using the evaluation form from the class to learn what they knew, learned, and want to learn. Pricing information could be gathered at this experimental class and substituted for extensive, outside market research.

Conclusions and Questions to Be Answered

1. There are many patrons' education needs which are not being met.

2. There are many methods to deliver education needs which could be self-directed by the patron on demand at their convenience.

3. Staff time will be needed to develop learning aids which then will be mechanisms to free staff from repetitive task.

4. Staff can be utilized to teach special classes which may provide job enrichment for patrons and increase their awareness of our services and library tool usage.

5. Short-term and longer-term solutions need to be identified and listed by priority.

6. Marketing needs to be targeted and begun in small increments.

APPENDIX B: EXAMPLE PROGRAM EVALUATION FORMS

FAIRFAX COUNTY PUBLIC LIBRARY

SEND TO PROGRAM COORDINATOR NO LATER THAN THE LAST OF THE MONTH

Program Title: _____

Day: _____ Date: _____ Time: _____

Attendance (count Target Audience only):

Single Program: _____

Series: _____ _____

_____ _____

_____ _____ Total: _____ Average Att. Per Program: _____

How many in each age group (count Target Audience only; approximate if necessary)

0-5 _____ 6-12 _____ YA _____ Adult _____ Seniors _____

If any organized groups attended, note the name of the group _____

and number of attendees: _____

Narrative Evaluation: What you did—best part, worst part, who came, quality of performer/co-sponsor, recommendations for future use of this program, etc.

Costs:

Staff Hours, Preparation: _____ × $10 = _____ Volunteer Hours: _____

Presentation: _____ × $10 = _____

Travel: _____ × $10 = _____

Materials and/or Performer Fee: _____

TOTAL $_____ divided by Attendance = COST PER ATTENDEE: $_____

Prepared by _____ Branch _____ Date _____

NORFOLK PUBLIC LIBRARY SYSTEM
USING PUBLIC LIBRARY RESOURCES

SESSION III   DATE: _____

    The third session of our course is designed to further enhance your understanding of the elements that make up a catalog card and your general use of the library.

    Please rate how well the course covered the following. Any comments you wish to make will be of great value—please feel free to make them in the allotted space, or in the margins, on the back, etc.

1. Classification and Call Numbers.

    Our objective is to explain the concept of library classification by examining a variety of call numbers you may encounter in a library.

       1   2   3   4   5   Comments:
     Very   Poorly
     well

2. Subject Headings.

    Our objective is to acquaint you with additional techniques for looking up a subject in the library catalog.

       1   2   3   4   5   Comments:
     Very   Poorly
     well

3. Techniques for locating materials.

    Our objective is to provide you with the opportunity to locate an item in our library, or if unable to locate it, to know why and what to do next.

       1   2   3   4   5   Comments:
     Very   Poorly
     well

4. New Technology.

    Our objective is to present a brief historical sketch leading up to present and future effects of automation and networking on libraries.

       1   2   3   4   5   Comments:
     Very   Poorly
     well

5. How new to you is the material covered in this session?

       1   2   3   4   5   Comments:
     Very   Very
     new   familiar

6. Instructor.

The intent of the instructor is to present the above material competently, and in an effective manner. Please rate the following:

a. Knowledge of subject matter.

    1   2   3   4   5   Comments:
  Very   Poorly
  well

b. Presentation.

    1   2   3   4   5   What did you like most?
  Very   Ineffec-
  effective   tive   What did you like least?

7. How useful to you is the material covered in this session?

    1   2   3   4   5   Comments:
  Very   Of little
  useful   use

8. Materials used.

The intent governing our selection of materials is to supplement the information we hope to convey, and to enhance our presentation. Please rate the following:

a. Text: "Your Library, What's in It for You?" Chapter 1.

    1   2   3   4   5   Comments:
  Very   Poor
  good

b. Glossary of library language.

    1   2   3   4   5   Comments:
  Very   Poor
  good

c. The card catalog unmasked.

    1   2   3   4   5   Comments:
  Very   Poor
  good

d. Visuals used with the overhead projector.

    1   2   3   4   5   Comments:
  Very   Poor
  good

Please feel free to use the remainder of this sheet for comments. Your signature is not required.

APPENDIX C: EXAMPLE OF PUBLIC LIBRARY COURSE OUTLINE AND ASSIGNMENT

Example of Public Library Course Outline

USING PUBLIC LIBRARY RESOURCES

Presented by the Norfolk Public Library course instructors.

The course is conducted in seven sessions of two and a half hours each, plus a one-hour lab.

I. FIRST SESSION

    A. Introduction.

    B. Tour of Kirn Memorial Library.

II. SECOND SESSION

    A. Catalog cards.

        1. Discussion of the elements that make up a catalog card.

        2. Discussion of the types of catalog cards for an item.

    B. Library catalog.

        1. Some of the filing arrangements found in the catalog.

        2. Call slips and locating material in the library.

    C. Discussion of three additional types of main entries.

        1. Corporate author.

        2. Title.

        3. Uniform title.

III. THIRD SESSION (Catalog interpretation continued).

    A. Classification and call numbers.

        1. Dewey Decimal classification.

        2. Library of Congress classification.

        3. Cuttering.

        4. Call numbers.

    B. Subject headings.

        1. Discussion of subject approach to library collections.

        2. Discussion and demonstration of patron use of the L.C. Subject Heading List.

    C. Booklet: *The Card Catalog Unmasked*.

        1. Discussion of problem-solving techniques the patron might use when searching for materials in the catalog and for books on the shelves.

    D. New technology.

        1. Automation.

        2. Networking.

    E. Practical work.

        1. Participants are asked to locate an assigned subject in the card catalog, then a book.

        2. A microfiche reader and samples of a CCM catalog on fiche are presented for examination.

IV. FOURTH SESSION

    A. Discussion of reference books.

        1. General reference books (dictionaries, encyclopedias, etc.

        2. Subject reference books (business directories, quotations handbooks, etc.).

    B. Discussion of vertical file.

    C. Discussion of government documents (federal, state, municipal).

    D. Interlibrary loans.

    E. Practical work.

        1. Participants prepare for class by reading a chapter in textbook and answering a reference question.

        2. During class discussion, reference books are examined by participants.

V. FIFTH SESSION (Periodicals)

    A. Discussion of periodicals.

        1. General.

        2. Professional journals.

    B. Discussion of indexes and library publishers.

        1. General indexes (*Readers' Guide*, etc.).

        2. Subject indexes (*Humanities Index, Business Index*, etc.).

    C. Practical work.

        1. Each participant is given a list of frequently used indexes and asked to locate answers to assigned questions.

VI. SIXTH SESSION (children's department, audiovisual).

    A. Discussion of resources of the children's department.

        1. Resources available.

        2. Techniques for their use.

    B. Discussion of audiovisual resources of the Feldman Audio-Visual Department.

        1. Materials available.

        2. Equipment.

VII. SEVENTH SESSION (Library and the community).

    A. Final tour of Kirn Memorial Library.

    B. Search strategies collected and discussed (required for teachers earning in-service credit unit; optional for other participants).

    C. Address by a library official.

    D. Library and the community.

        1. Community outreach.

        2. Schools and school library resources.

            a. Description of central resource centers of Norfolk.

**Example of Public Library
Course Assignment**

NORFOLK PUBLIC LIBRARY SYSTEM
"USING PUBLIC LIBRARY RESOURCES"

SEARCH STRATEGY

Topic _____

Name_____Date_____

    Select and initial a topic from the posted list. If you have a topic of your own, clear it with an instructor before proceeding.

    Plan a search strategy for your topic using Norfolk Public Library resources to answer the questions below. Your purpose is to identify resources containing information on your topic, *not* to collect the actual information.

1. Card Catalog

    List 2 bibliographical citations on your topic.

    (1) Call number _____

         Main entry _____

         Title _____

         Publisher _____

         Date _____

    (2) Call number _____

         Main entry _____

         Title _____

         Publisher _____

         Date _____

Name 3 subject headings for your topic.

    (1) _____

    (2) _____

    (3) _____

2. Reference Books

    Select 3 classes of reference tools listed below. Name one title per class which contains information on your topic.

    Classes: Dictionaries, encyclopedias, almanacs, atlases, manuals, handbooks, yearbooks, directories.

    (1) Class _____

         Title _____

SEARCH STRATEGY   TOPIC _____   Page _____

    (2) Class _____

          Title _____

    (3) Class _____

          Title _____

3. Vertical File

Consult a librarian for vertical file information on your topic.

    (1) Name the library department in which you searched.

        _____

    (2) List the heading under which information on your topic was filed in the vertical file.

        _____

4. Documents (federal, state, municipal)

Find information on your topic in a federal document.

    (1) _____

Find information on your topic in a state *or* municipal document.

    (1) _____

5. Periodicals

Search 2 separate indexes to periodicals for information on your topic. Name the indexes you searched.

    (1) _____

    (2) _____

Cite at least 3 references you found.

    (1) Title of periodical (abbreviate) _____

        Volume number of periodical _____

        Page numbers of article _____

        Date of periodical _____

    (2) Title of periodical (abbreviate) _____

        Volume number of periodical _____

        Page numbers of article _____

        Date of periodical _____

SEARCH STRATEGY   TOPIC _____   Page _____

    (3) Title of periodical (abbreviate) _____

          Volume number of periodical _____

          Page numbers of article _____

          Date of periodical _____

6. Children's Department Materials

List at least 3 items from the children's department containing information on your topic.

    (1) Call number _____

          Main entry _____

          Title _____

    (2) Call number _____

          Main entry _____

          Title _____

    (3) Call number _____

          Main entry _____

          Title _____

7. Audiovisual Materials

List 3 nonbook items which relate to your topic.

Items: Pictures, prints, sculpture, posters, 16mm films, 8mm films, filmstrips, slides, cassettes, phonodiscs, kits, transparencies, and additional nonbook items.

    (1) Call number _____

          Main entry _____

          Title _____

    (2) Call number _____

          Main entry _____

          Title _____

    (3) Call number _____

          Main entry _____

          Title _____

APPENDIX D: EXAMPLES
OF PUBLIC LIBRARY
INSTRUCTION PUBLICITY

TEACHERS

enhance your use of

THE PUBLIC LIBRARY

and earn

ONE IN-SERVICE CREDIT

* *

WINTER 1986

USING PUBLIC LIBRARY RESOURCES

COURSE APPLICATION FORM

NORFOLK PUBLIC LIBRARY SYSTEM

Keeping up with the information explosion can be a challenge. Librarians of the Norfolk Public Library System have designed a course to help you keep in touch with what is available.

Topics covered include the catalog card, library classification, subject searching, a wide variety of reference materials, use of periodical indexes, and introduction to A-V materials and new technology available in many libraries, and more. Teachers in the NPSS may earn one in-service credit.

The seven-session course will be taught by librarians at Kirn Memorial Library, 301 E. City Hall Ave. in three sections: seven Saturday mornings (10-12:30) starting February 1; or seven Tuesday mornings (10-12:30) starting February 4; or seven Thursday evenings (6:30-9) starting February 6. The course is also offered to other library users. It is designed for adults, but interested high school students are welcome.

REGISTRATION DEADLINE: JANUARY 25. Must be accompanied by a *nonrefundable $10.00 fee* covering registration and text. Checks payable to NORFOLK PUBLIC LIBRARY SYSTEM. Upon successful completion, teachers may apply for a $5.00 refund from the Office of Human Relations and Staff Development. Questions? CALL 441-2426 Monday-Friday between 9:30 a.m. and 3 p.m.

-- cut here --

MAIL TO: LIBRARY COURSE INSTRUCTORS, NORFOLK PUBLIC LIBRARY SYSTEM
           301 E. City Hall Avenue, Norfolk, Virginia 23510   Winter 1986

NAME: _____   HOME PHONE:_____

HOME ADDRESS: _____   BUSINESS PHONE: _____

           _____   SCHOOL NAME: _____

SECTION (CHOOSE ONE):

SATURDAYS_____   TUESDAYS_____   THURSDAYS_____
(10-12:30)   (10-12:30)   (6:30-9)

The City of San Diego
San Diego Public Library
820 E Street
San Diego, California 92101

Invitation to

Members of the
Board of Library Commissioners

San Diego Friends of the Public Library

Special Librarians of San Diego

and

Serra System Librarians

Seventh in the Series of Inside Looks

at Central Library Subject Sections

An Inside Look at History and World Affairs Section

On Wednesday, June 24

At 8:40 a.m. - 9:30 a.m.

In History Section on First Floor
of Central Library
(enter Eighth Avenue entrance to Library)

Reception following in Commission Room
9:30 a.m. - 10:00 a.m.

R.S.V.P. by Friday, June 19

BIBLIOGRAPHY

General

Amason, Craig R. "Instruction for Genealogists in the Public Library." *Reference Librarian* 22 (1988): 283-95.

Batt, F. "Bibliographic Instruction (B.I.): Examination of Changing Emphasis." In *Advances in Library Administration and Organization*, edited by Gerard B. McCabe and Bernard Kreissman, vol. 5. Greenwich, Conn.: Jai Press, 1986.

Beilke, Patricia F. "Library Instruction in Public Libraries: A Dream Deferred, A Goal to Actualize." *Reference Librarian* 10 (Spring/Summer 1984): 123-33.

Bingham, K. H., and Loomis, A. A. "Library Instruction for Special User Groups." *Illinois Libraries* 70 (December 1988): 627-76.

Carbone, Jerry. "Library Use Instruction in the Small and Medium Public Library: A Review of the Literature." *Reference Librarian* 10 (Spring/Summer 1984): 149-57.

Detrich, Jerrolyn M. "Library Use Instruction for Older Adults." *Canadian Library Journal* 41 (August 1984): 203-8.

Hendley, Margaret. "User Education: The Adult Patron in the Public Library." *RQ* 24 (Winter 1984): 291-94.

Kinney, Elaine M. "Thirty Minutes and Counting: A Bibliographic Instruction Program." *Illinois Libraries* 70 (January 1988): 36-37.

Kohl, David F. *Reference Services and Library Instruction.* Santa Barbara, Calif.: ABC-Clio, 1985.

Lubens, John, Jr., compiler and editor. *Educating the Public Library User.* Chicago: American Library Association, 1983.

Reichel, Mary, and Mary Ann Ramey, eds. *Conceptual Framework for Bibliographic Education: Theory into Practice.* Littleton, Colo.: Libraries Unlimited, Inc., 1987.

Reilly, Jane A. "Library Instruction through the Reference Query." *Reference Librarian* 10 (Spring/Summer 1984): 135-48.

Shih, T. C. *Library Instruction: A Bibliography, 1975 through 1985.* New York: McFarland & Co., 1986.

Handbooks and Manuals on Library Instruction

Breivik, Patricia F. *Planning the Library Instruction Program.* Chicago: American Library Association, 1982.

Roberts, Anne F., and Susan G. Blandy. *Library Instruction for Librarians,* 2nd rev. ed. Englewood, Colo.: Libraries Unlimited, Inc., 1989.

Needs Assessment

Givens, Johnnie E. "User Instruction: Assessing Needs for the Future." In *Library Instruction and Reference Services,* edited by Bill Katz and Ruth Fraley. New York: Haworth Press, 1984.

Glover, Peggy D. *Library Services for the Woman in the Middle.* Hamden, Conn.: Shoe String Press, 1985.

Kulthau, C. C. "Stages in Child and Adolescent Development and Implications for Library Instruction Programs." In *Information Seeking: Basing Services on Users' Behaviors,* edited by Jana Varlejs. New York: McFarland & Co., 1987.

McClure, Charles R. et al. *Planning & Role Setting for Public Libraries.* Chicago: American Library Association, 1987.

Oklahoma Department of Libraries. *Performance Measures for Oklahoma Public Libraries.* Oklahoma Department of Libraries, 1982.

Van House, Nancy A. et al. *Output Measures for Public Libraries.* Chicago: American Library Association, 1987.

Material and Methods

Clark, Alice S., and Kay F. Jones, ed. *Teaching Librarians to Teach: On-the-Job Training for Bibliographic Instruction Librarians.* Metuchen, N.J.: Scarecrow Press, 1986.

FitzGerald, P. et al. "Computer-Assisted Instruction in Libraries: Guidelines for Effective Lesson Design." *Library High Technology* 4 (Summer 1986): 29-37.

Knowles, Malcolm. *Self-Directed Learning: A Guide for Learners and Teachers.* New York: Press Association, 1975.

Kulthau, C. C. *Teaching the Library Research Process, A Step-by-Step Program for Secondary School Students.* West Nyack, N.Y.: Center for Applied Research in Education, Inc., 1985.

Lynch, Mary Jo. "Library Tours: The First Step." In *Educating the Library User*, edited by John Lubans, 254-68. New York: R. R. Bowker Company, 1983.

Malley, Ian. *The Basics of Information Skills Teaching*. London: Clive Bingley, 1984.

Paterson, E. R. "Just-for-Fun Quizzes Encourage Student Participation in Library Instruction." *Unabashed Librarian* 52 (1984): 3-4.

Pollet, Dorothy, and Peter C. Haskell. *Sign Systems for Librarians: Solving the Way-Finding Problem*. New York: R. R. Bowker Company, 1979.

Reilly, Jane A. "Library Instruction through the Reference Query." *Library Instruction and Reference Services*, edited by Bill Katz and Ruth A. Fraley, 135-48. New York: Haworth Press, 1984.

Roberts, Anne. "How to Generate User Interest in Library Orientation and Instruction." *Bookmark* 30 (Fall 1979): 228-30.

Roberts, Anne. "Teaching Librarians to Teach." *Lifeline* 17 (September 1981): 6-7.

Tessmer, M. "Applications of Instruction Design to Library Instruction." *Colorado Libraries* 11 (December 1985): 28-31.

Targeting the Audience

Dietrick, Jerrolyn M. "Library Use Instruction for Older Adults." *Canadian Library Journal* (August 1984): 203-8.

Evaluation

Beeler, Richard J., ed. *Evaluating Libraries Use Instruction (Denver Conference on the Evaluation of Library Instruction, December 13-14, 1973)*. Ann Arbor, Mich.: Pierian Press, 1975. (Library Orientation series, 4.)

Kirkendall, Carolyn. *Improving Library Instruction: How to Teach and How to Evaluate (Conference on Library Orientation for Academic Libraries, 8th, Eastern Michigan University, 1978)*. Ann Arbor, Mich.: Pierian Press, 1979 (published for the Center of Educational Resources).

Vogel, J. Thomas. "A Critical Overview for Evaluation of Library Instruction." *Drexel Library Quarterly* 8 (July 1972): 315-23.

Resources—Games

Bell, Irene Wood, and Jeanne E. Wieckert. *Basic Media Skills through Games*. 2nd ed. Littleton, Colo.: Libraries Unlimited, Inc., 1985.

Bragg, James. *Screwy Dewey [boardgame]*. Ottawa: Canadian Library Association, 1980.

Karpisek, Marian E. *Making Self-Teaching Kits for Library Skills*. Chicago: American Library Association, 1983.

Lewis, Zella, comp. *Developing Learning Skills through Library Services K-12*. Chicago: American Library Association/Library Instruction Round Table, 1981. (Available from ERIC Document Reproduction Services ED 211 095.)

Mallet, Jerry J., and Marian R. Bartch. *Elementary School Library Resource Kit (K-12)*. West Nyack, N.Y.: Center for Applied Research in Education, Inc., 1984.

Programming with Interpretive Activities. Chicago: American Library Association/Association for Library Services for Children, 1982.

PART IV
SCHOOL LIBRARIES

Instruction in the Use of Library Media Centers in Schools

Fran Corcoran
School District 62
Des Plaines, Illinois

Dianne Langlois
Andrew Mellon Library
Choate Rosemary Hall
Wallingford, Connecticut

INTRODUCTION

If 90 percent of the knowledge known to man by 2025 will have been discovered since 1978, then our future leaders' needs are for information gathering skills, not just the information itself.* School library media specialists have always viewed teaching students how to identify, retrieve, and use library media center resources effectively as their principal function. With the library media center as their classroom, school library media specialists are uniquely qualified and situated to develop programs to teach students information skills. Traditionally, library media specialists have used the term "library skills" program to describe their instructional efforts. In light of technological and curricular advances, "information skills" program is the more descriptive term. Since information skills are the foundation for independent life-long learning, it is vital that students master them.

The goal of an information skills program is to teach students information gathering strategies so they can identify, retrieve and use needed materials for both immediate and long-term academic and personal needs. The most successful information skills programs are taught as an integral part of the school's basic curriculum. This focus assumes an academic need—a classroom correlation. Information skills programs thrive in an academic environment where the following assumptions are made:

1. The administration views the library media specialist as a teacher and the information gathering skills as a necessary part of every student's education.

2. Subject area curricula include the appropriate information gathering and usage skills as part of the behavioral objectives.

3. The superintendent and the principals encourage team planning by teacher and library media specialist.

4. Evaluation of the program is an annual event in order to keep the information skills curriculum fresh and current with curricular changes.

---

*White House Conference 1978 film "For What Do We Plan."

In this less than perfect world, many library media specialists find themselves in situations which do not reflect the above assumptions/support. Because information skills are crucial, library media specialists cannot abdicate their responsibility to teach students information skills. Library media specialists, without support, must simply be more creative and face the challenge of instructing students with an informal program. Informal programs take as much thought and planning as formal programs, so the techniques outlined in this chapter apply equally to formal and informal information skills programs.

Even though school librarianship has information skills instruction as a fundamental tenet, academic librarians are heard to claim that students are arriving at the nation's colleges and universities with only the barest understanding of how to retrieve and use information from library media centers. While many attribute this state of affairs to the general decline of primary and secondary education, others charge that the basic design of the instruction programs is at fault. Since the truth probably rests somewhere in-between, school library media specialists with existing instructional programs, as well as library media specialists designing new ones, need to spend time analyzing instructional design and method to determine how their programs can be made more effective.

The following sources provide more information on assumptions regarding library skills programs:

Library Media Specialist as Teacher

Information Power: Guidelines for School Library Media Programs. Chicago: American Library Association, 1988.

McDonald, Frances Beck, ed. *The Emerging School Library Media Program: Readings.* Englewood, Colo.: Libraries Unlimited, Inc., 1988.

Wehmeyer, Lillian Biermann. *The School Librarian as Educator.* 2nd ed. Littleton, Colo.: Libraries Unlimited, Inc., 1984.

Information Gathering Skills Necessary for All Students

The College Board. *Academic Preparation for College.* New York: The College Board, 1983.

Hart, Thomas L., ed. *Instruction in School Media Center Use.* Chicago: American Library Association, 1978, 123-29.

Haycock, Carol-Ann. "Information Skills in the Curriculum: Developing a School Based Continuum." *Emergency Librarian* 13 (September-October 1985): 11-17.

Kuhlthau, Carol Collier. "Meeting the Information Needs of Children and Young Adults: Basing Library Media Programs on Developmental States." *Journal of Youth Services in Libraries* 2 (Fall 1988): 51-57.

Kuhlthau, Carol Collier. *Teaching the Library Research Process: A Step-by-Step Program for Secondary School Students.* West Nyack, N.Y.: Center for Applied Research in Education, Inc., 1985.

Lewis, Marguerite, and Pamela Kudla. *Hooked on Library Skills.* West Nyack, N.Y.: Center for Applied Research in Education, Inc., 1988.

Polette, Nancy. *Research without Copying.* O'Fallon, Mo.: Book Lures, 1988.

Snoddon, Ruth V. *Library Skills Activities for Primary Grades.* West Nyack, N.Y.: Center for Applied Research in Education, Inc., 1987.

Subject Area Curriculum Including Appropriate Information Gathering

Computer Ideabook: Computer Activities for Basic Subjects Grades 3-8. New York: Scholastic, 1985.

Davies, Ruth Ann. *The School Library Media Center: A Force for Educational Excellence.* 2nd ed. New York: R. R. Bowker Company, 1974, 257-58.

Gillespie, John T., and Diana L. Spirt. *Creating a School Media Program.* New York: R. R. Bowker Company, 1973, 29-31, 36.

Leopold, Carolyn Clugston. *School Libraries Worth Their Keep: A Philosophy Plus Tricks.* Metuchen, N.J.: Scarecrow Press, 1972, 257-58.

Toor, Ruth, and Hilda K. Weisburg. *Sharks, Ships and Potato Chips: Curriculum Integrated Library Instruction.* Berkeley Heights, N.J.: Library Learning Resources, Inc., 1986.

Teacher and Library Media Center Team in Eyes of Superintendent and Principal

A Guide to School Library Media Programs. Hartford, Conn.: Connecticut State Board of Education, 1982, 9-12.

Hart, Thomas L., ed. *Instruction in School Media Center Use.* Chicago: American Library Association, 1978, 24-26.

Yesner, B. L., and H. L. Jay. *The School Administration's Guide to Evaluating Library Media Programs.* Hamden, Conn.: Shoe String Press, 1987.

Teacher and Library Media Specialist as a Team

Bradstad, Bernice Jensen, and Sharyn Mueller Stumpf. *A Guidebook for Teaching Study Skills and Motivation.* 2nd ed. Boston: Allyn and Bacon, 1987, chapter 10.

Devine, Thomas. *Teaching Study Skills: A Guide for Teachers.* Boston: Allyn and Bacon, 1987.

Haycock, Ken, and Carol-Ann Haycock. *Kids and Libraries.* Seattle, Wash.: Dyad Services, 1984.

Information Power. Chicago: American Library Association: American Association of School Librarians and the Association for Educational Communications and Technology, 1988.

Irving, Ann. *Study and Information/Skills across the Curriculum.* London: Heinemann Educational Books, 1985.

Procedures Manual for School Library Media Centers. Oklahome: Oklahoma State Department of Education, 1982.

NEEDS ASSESSMENT

Unfortunately for library information skill instruction, most library media specialists start with program design rather than gathering information via a needs assessment. Library media specialists proceed this way because they do not feel they have time to do a proper needs assessment. How does one go about assessing student needs? Processes of assessment include formal surveys of students' needs and informal observations regarding how the patrons use the library independently. A thorough needs assessment also includes an analysis of the student population with regards to general academic level, expectations, and socioeconomic background.

When undertaking a needs assessment study, start with the curriculum guide or textbook. There will be many opportunities for increasing information gathering and usage skills built into its learning activities. Curriculum guides indicate where and when such skills are required. A careful study of course descriptions indicates the type of information skills students need to successfully complete their academic program. For example, if the student is required to write a report on deserts, that student should know what sources are available and how to access and use the various informational formats. As the library media specialist goes through the school curriculum, he or she will be able to identify informational skills which are required at each grade level. A careful reading of the guides will also indicate when a preskill is required—such as alphabetizing for index or card catalog use, note taking to avoid plagiarism, or analysis of opinion versus fact sources—before a research project, and these skills should be noted. The information skills demanded by the academic curriculum represent the actual information needs of your students.

Pretests can also provide a picture of students' information needs. The library media specialist can create an original test, adapt another library media center's test, or use a commercially available test. *Minimum Library Use Skills: Standards Test, and Bibliography*, available from Wisconsin Library Association, is a useful model for anyone creating a pretest. With the appearance of microcomputers in library media centers, it may be possible to prepare a test using the computer. This would simplify creating and grading the test.

Another approach for assessing needs is to survey students to determine which skills they are using or not using. One survey simply asked students to list where they would find information on a typical student question, such as, "Where would you find information on Martin Luther King?" Another asked students to answer a six-question survey indicating which standard sources they used after they were given a research topic. Still another library media specialist asked students to judge two different sources for usefulness. These types of surveys can reveal the resources with which the students are most familiar. This data is valuable because underutilization of resources may be the result of lack of understanding about how to find and use them. These assessment methods allow teaching library media specialists to identify specific research tools which should be addressed.

While needs assessment should not be limited to the library media specialist's observation, the value of this method should not be underestimated. Keeping a log of students' questions provides a clear indication of what they do not understand about using the library media center. If students ask for help in translating citations from indexes, the library media specialist will know that more time needs to be spent explaining the parts of a citation. In a similar manner, if students constantly complain that the library media center has no books on a subject, when books are actually available, students are not using the catalog properly. In this case, a lesson on using the catalog to find books when only a subject is known may be required. Students may be in the habit of using the first three sources they find on a topic. This may require guidance on how to be a discriminating user of information.

Although another library media center's experience is not completely transferable to your own situation, it can help highlight similar situations. A literature search can uncover clues to possible student and faculty needs. Current library journals often deal with new research, while books devoted to managing an information skills program detail model skills curricula. The major library and education indexes are invaluable for identifying relevant references.

In addition to a clear understanding of what type of information skills students need and what skills they actually possess, a complete needs assessment will seek to define students as learners. To do this, the library media specialist will need to know the answers to the following questions:

- What is the students' current level of general knowledge?

- How motivated are they to learn about the library media center?

- What is their attention span likely to be?

- Which teaching techniques will be most successful?

- What are the students' special interests?

The best ways to gain this information is to look over standard test scores that profile the students as learners, review samples of students' written work, and talk with teachers. Check with the administrative offices of the school to see if statistical data related to socioeconomic status is available. This type of data will yield insight into the students' environments and their possible attitudes towards school and the library media center. Attitudes about the library media center and information skill instruction are very important because they determine in large measure the students' motivational level.

With all the recent changes in library media centers brought about by technology, a school's teaching staff is often not fully aware of the range of relevant media and how to make the best use of it. Teachers also have information needs which should be identified so they can be addressed. Library media specialists should apply the principle of needs assessment—formal and informal surveys, observation, and review of statistical data—to the teaching faculty at their school. A library media specialist who is working to develop an integrated program may want to concentrate on faculty needs in the beginning. If the teachers are not convinced of the value of information skills, they may unwittingly transmit negative attitudes to their students.

Needs assessment should be seen as a continuous process undertaken periodically to maintain a clear picture of student needs. For it is the search for this kind of information which constantly sharpens the library media specialist's view of what students know, what they need to know, and how best they will learn. This picture will allow program design to follow logically. Without the needs assessment, program planning has very little chance of being successful for the simple reason that the library media specialist has no well-founded idea what should be taught to which group.

For more information on needs assessment see:

Fields, Carolyn B. "Using Results of a Pre-Test to Determine Lecture Content: A Case Study." *Research Strategies* 5 (1987): 29-35.

Freedman, Janet L., and Harold A. Bantly. *Information Searching: A Handbook for Designing and Creating Instructional Programs.* Rev. ed. Metuchen, N.J.: Scarecrow Press, 1982, 6-13.

Patrick, Retta B. "Information Power: The Planning Process." *School Library Media Quarterly* 17 (Winter 1989): 88a-88k.

"Why Ideas Fail: These Students Need to Know This." *Learning Today* (Summer 1980): 24-25.

Wisconsin Library Association. *Minimum Library Use Skills: Standard Test and Bibliography.* Madison, Wis.: Wisconsin Library Association, n.d.

DETERMINING INFORMATION SKILL CURRICULUM

Students must acquire three types of information skills in order to meet the information demands placed on them by their school work. The first type of skill, called a resource skill, deals with exploiting individual resources, for example, how to use the catalog to locate and retrieve the materials desired. The second type of skill is more sophisticated and builds on the first type; it entails learning how to employ resources as part of a systematic search strategy to solve research problems. Identifying and using a standard bibliography to create a working bibliography is an example of this research skill. The third skill requires that students know what to do with information once it has been gathered.

Having completed a thorough needs assessment that identified the information students need to successfully meet their academic curriculum, the library media specialist must translate these information needs into an information skills curriculum. Satisfying a single information need defined in the assessment usually requires mastery of several information skills. If the school curriculum mandates that students write papers on foreign elections in a current events course, the student will need the following skills: locate *The Readers' Guide*; generate appropriate subject headings; understand filing rules; decode the parts of a periodical citation; and retrieve the correct periodical issue, which may require the use of periodical holdings lists and the microform readers.

At first, library media specialists may find it difficult to break down information needs into discrete information skills because they are so familiar with library media center resources that they take for granted the variety of skills required to effectively use those resources. It is very important that all necessary skills are identified, because it is these skills that will be adopted as behavioral objectives for actual instructional sessions. Library media specialists must also be sensitive to the preskills that are required before another skill can be executed. Des Plaines [Illinois] District 62 Study Skills includes note-taking beginning in the third grade, so that by the time the sixth-grade research project is given, students will have well-developed note-taking skills.

As students' information needs become more sophisticated, the instruction focus naturally moves away from specific resource skills to research skills. For instance, a child needing information on caring for a new puppy will have the subject heading in his vocabulary. However, the high school student doing a report on the "red scare" will probably have to do background reading to generate subject headings for that topic. The ability to generate subject terms is one of the research skills students need to learn to acquire information. On a third level, students must be able to choose and be critical of the information they locate. Copyright date may be a significant factor. Can they ascertain the difference between fact and opinion? Can they scan information sources quickly for relevant information? Can they organize ideas from numerous sources into a coherent pattern as the basis of a paper?

Listing all the information skills needed by a specific grade level and then breaking down the skills into resource and search strategy skills can be a time-consuming and difficult task. The library media specialist creating a program should take advantage of library media center information skills curricular guides that have already been developed. These documents are usually generated at the district or state level, or they can be found in books which deal with teaching library media center skills. The ERIC indexes are useful to identify recent curricular guides. By consulting existing skill curricula, library media specialists can check their assumptions against programs that have evolved over a period of time. At the same time, it is important to remember that no library media center can adopt another's curriculum exactly. Local conditions must dictate the final curriculum for a particular area.

The process of determining the information skill curriculum can be summarized with the following:

MOVING FROM IDENTIFIED
INFORMATION NEEDS TO INFORMATION
REQUIRED BY THE CURRICULUM TO
SKILLS STUDENTS SHOULD ACQUIRE,
I.E., SKILL OBJECTIVES

The curriculum requires that the student reads a biography and prepares a book report.
(INFORMATION NEED)

So, students need to be able to find an appropriate biography in the school library.
(LOCATIONAL SKILL)

Which means students must acquire all of the following skills:
(SKILL OBJECTIVES)

1. Can use the card catalog or computer catalog to identify biographies. (This assumes understanding that a name can be a subject, or the ability to formulate other subject headings which are used for biographies.)

2. Can locate the call number on catalog card or record.

3. Can use the call number to find the book on the shelf.

4. Can make a judgment about the usefulness of one or several biographies found.

Once the information needs are broken down into clear skills objectives, the library media specialist should get together with the classroom teacher to determine how the objective will be taught. Will the library media specialist introduce it and the teacher reinforce it, or the other way around? A team teaching approach is desirable. Barbara Bradley Zlotnick's book, *Ready for Reference*, outlines a classic program of fully integrated information skill instructions.

For more information on determining information skill objectives see:

Hart, Thomas L., ed. *Instruction in School Media Center Use.* Chicago: American Library Association, 1978, 123-24.

Kolner, Bernard G., and Joan B. Meyers. *Key Competencies. Libraries: Elementary, Junior High, Senior High.* Philadelphia: Philadelphia School District, 1980.

Stripling, Barbara K., and Judy M. Pitts. *Brainstorms and Blueprints: Teaching Library Research as a Thinking Process.* Englewood, Colo.: Libraries Unlimited, Inc., 1988.

The Wisconsin Library Media Skill Guide. Madison, Wis.: Wisconsin Library Association, 1979.

Zlotnick, Barbara Bradley. *Ready for Reference: Media Skills for Intermediate Students.* Littleton, Colo.: Libraries Unlimited, Inc., 1984.

LESSON DESIGN

The first step in lesson design is to identify the target group. Once the group has been selected, review its information needs and learning characteristics as charted in the needs assessment. It is important to recognize that each group of learners is different. By carefully considering the group's learning style and information needs, the library media specialist can design a lesson based on skill objectives that fit the needs, interests, and knowledge level of the group being taught. The skill objective, written in behavioral language, notes the desired behavior outcome. For example, that the student will be able to identify and translate a citation found in the *Readers' Guide to Periodical Literature.*

In her writings on elements of effective lesson design, Madeline Hunter outlines a heuristic method for achieving well-planned lessons. The seven considerations for every lesson plan include:

1. ANTICIPATORY SET

   Do I need to (a) get attention, (b) start class to thinking (focus), or (c) practice information which will be used?

2. OBJECTIVE

   What is my objective? Do I tell students or develop it during the lesson? How?

3. INPUT

   What information do I need to provide? Review? New? How?

4. MODELING

   What examples, models, illustrations, etc., should I use?

5. CHECKING FOR UNDERSTANDING

   What do I want children to be able to do? How will I check?

6. GUIDED PRACTICE

   Will they need to practice something? If so, what? How?

7. INDEPENDENT PRACTICE

   Will I need to give an independent practice assignment? What? How much? How will they know if they are doing it right?

Library media specialists must be more sensitive to students' learning styles. Research has shown the teacher usually unconsciously prepares the lesson in a way he or she learns best, so the other styles can be met only by conscious planning. In the Des Plaines schools, both teachers and children have been profiled as to their learning styles using the Dunn definitions. The teachers are expected to incorporate learning experiences in daily lessons to accommodate the learning style needs of their students. Research concerning left- and right-brained learners emphasizes the need for variety in teaching methods and learner expectations. This variety—using auditory, visual, and kinesthetic modalities—is part of Hunter's focus on modeling (see step 4) and can be included in practice options. The evaluation of the learning or changed behavior is built into the lesson design under step 5 (checking for understanding).

For more information on lesson design see:

Barth, Marian R., and Jerry J. Mallett. *Reading Roussers: 114 Ways to Reading Fun.* Santa Monica, Calif.: Goodyear Publishing Co., Inc., 1980.

Kulthau, Carol Collier. "A Process Approach to Library Skills Instruction." *School Library Media Quarterly* 13 (Winter 1985): 35-40.

Miller, Marian I., and Barry D. Bratton. "Instructional Design: Increasing the Effectiveness of Bibliographic Instruction." *College & Research Libraries* 49 (November 1988): 545-49.

Peterson, Lorna. "Ask a Silly Question: Responses from Library Instruction Quizzes." *Research Strategies* 6 (Winter 1988): 25-28.

Tuckett, Harold W., and Carla J. Stoffle. "Learning Theory and the Self-Reliant Library User." *RQ* 24 (Fall 1984): 58-66.

Turner, Philip M. *Helping Teachers Teach: A School Library/ Media Specialist's Role.* Littleton, Colo.: Libraries Unlimited, Inc., 1985.

PROGRAM OPTIONS

There is no single, self-evident, or absolutely right way to instruct library media center users. It is important to remember that few perfect programs are created. Most successful programs have evolved and improved over a period of time. What follows are general approaches to library media center information skill instruction. While most programs are a hybrid of several methods, they are listed separately to clearly spell out the advantages and disadvantages of each. A reference to an article dealing with that method follows most descriptions. Finally, closing this section is a list of references which deal with complete programs. Many of these ideas come from librarians not in a school situation. Do not overlook these articles. Good ideas from other situations can easily be adapted.

Orientation Methods

Signage—a systematic effort to provide students with directional, instructional, and identification signs.

Advantage:	signs are available even when library staff is busy; signs answer questions students are reluctant to ask; signs can reinforce instruction by reminding students what resources exist or how to use a resource.
Disadvantage:	requires planning and budget; needs to be updated and maintained.

For more information on signage see:

Kupersmith, John. "Information Graphics and Sign Systems as Library Instruction Media." *Drexel Library Quarterly* 16 (January 1980): 54-68.

Mallery, Mary S., and Ralph E. De Vore. *A Sign System for Libraries.* Chicago: American Library Association, 1982.

Piech, Carol R., Mary K. Delmont, and G. Charles Newman. "Butler Library Displays Vital Signs: Signage as a Remedy for Environmental Problems." *College & Research Libraries News* 47 (June 1986): 379-81.

Self-guided tour—students are guided by a printed map, a marked route, and/or a tape recorder.

Advantage:	introduces students to library layout and resources at a time convenient to the student; does not require the librarian to give the same speech repeatedly.
Disadvantage:	everyone gets the same instruction regardless of need; students cannot get immediate feedback by asking questions; students are often distracted and retain little that is presented.

For more information on self-guided tours see:

Chaffin, Jeff. "Macintosh-assisted Library Orientation Tour." *College & Research Libraries News* 48 (June 1987): 332-34.

Guided tour—students are guided by other students, library staff, volunteers, or librarians.

Advantage:	introduces student to library layout and sets a friendly tone which encourages future questions; allows immediate feedback.
Disadvantage:	difficult to ensure quality control from group to group; by the nature of the method, the presentation is oversimplified; students are often distracted and retain little of what is presented.

For more information on guided tours see:

Lawton, Bethany, and Ann Pederson. "Cue Cards Clues: A New Approach to Library Orientation." *Research Strategies* 6 (Spring 1988): 77-79.

Slide/tapes or videotapes—students can be given an overview of the entire library media center, or a program can be tailored to teach a specific skill or resource.

Advantage:	students respond well to media presentations; good method for handling large number of students as well as an individual student; allows the library media center to come to the classroom.

Disadvantage: can be time consuming and expensive to prepare; requires some technical skills; requires frequent updating.

For more information on visual orientation options see:

Foster, Barbara. "Do-It-Yourself Videotape for Library Orientation Based on a Term Paper Project." *Wilson Library Bulletin* 48 (February 1974): 476-81.

French, Nancy, and H. Jolene Butler. "Quiet on the Set! Library Instruction Goes Video." *Wilson Library Bulletin* 63 (December 1988): 42-44.

Garvey, Mona. *Library Public Relations: A Practical Handbook.* New York: H. W. Wilson, 1980.

Harper, J. E., and S. J. Tully. *Primary Library Activities.* Vancouver, B.C.: British Columbia Teachers' Federation, 1981.

Hauschild, Ruth, and Bettye Wilson. *Library Skills Grades 3-8.* Wheeling, Ill.: Community Consolidated School District 21, 1982.

Printed handouts — variety of types to meet different needs, for example, maps, bibliographies, pathfinders, research guides.

Advantage: inexpensive to create and update, especially with computer word processing; can be tailored to a specific group's needs; user can retain handout; can reinforce what is presented in program or stands alone as a teaching tool.

Disadvantage: difficult to present complex concepts; requires good design to be appealing; must be brief or students will ignore.

For more information on printed handouts see:

Canfield, Marie P. "Library Pathfinders." *Drexel Library Quarterly* 8 (July 1972): 287-300.

Christou, Corilee. "Marketing the Information Center: A Blue Print for Action." *Wilson Library Bulletin* 63 (April 1988): 35-37.

Edsall, Marian S. *Library Promotion Handbook.* Phoenix, Ariz.: Oryx Press, 1980.

Jackson, William. "The User-Friendly Library Guide." *College & Research Libraries News* 45 (October 1984): 468-71.

Stevens, Charles R., and Jeffrey J. Gardner. "Point of Use Library Instruction." In John Lubans, *Educating the Library User.* New York: R. R. Bowker Company, 1974.

Thompson, Glenn J., and Barbara R. Stevens. "Library Science Students Develop Pathfinders." *College & Research Libraries News* 46 (May 1985): 224-25.

Formal Methods of Instruction

Skills workbook — students are taught step by step about the library media center through workbook readings and assignments.

Advantage: the workbook can be self-paced; progress can be monitored through workbook assignment; commercial workbooks are available; can teach research strategy.

Disadvantage: user must be motivated; workbooks require updating; commercial products rarely reflect individual library media centers accurately; workbooks are time consuming and expensive to prepare; no immediate feedback.

For more information on skills workbooks see:

Donovan, Melissa. *Research Challenges: Through the Use of the Atlas, the Almanac, and Other World Resources.* Carthage, Ill.: Good Apple, Inc., 1985.

Graves, Gail, and Barbara K. Adams. "Bibliographic Instruction Workbooks: Assessing Two Models Used in a Freshman English Program." *Research Strategies* 6 (Winter 1988): 18-24.

Harper, J. E., and S. J. Tully. *Primary Library Activities.* Vancouver, B.C.: British Columbia Teachers' Federation, 1981.

Instructor's Big Book of Study Skills Reproducibles. New York: Instructor Books, 1983.

Karpisek, Marian E. *Making Self-teaching Kits for Library Skills.* Chicago: American Library Association, 1983.

Lewis, Marguerite. *Hooked on Research.* West Nyack, N.Y.: Center for Applied Research in Education, Inc., 1984.

Seaver, Alice R. *Library Media Skills: Strategies for Instructing Primary Students.* Littleton, Colo.: Libraries Unlimited, Inc., 1984.

Van Vliet, Lucille W. *Media Skills for Middle Schools: Strategies for Library Media Specialists and Teachers.* Littleton, Colo.: Libraries Unlimited, Inc., 1984.

Weisburg, Hilda K., and Ruth Toor. *Teachers Portfolio of Library Skills, Lessons and Activities.* West Nyack, N.Y.: Center for Applied Research in Education, Inc., 1985.

Wishau, Jan. *Investigator: A Guide for Independent Study Projects*. San Luis Obispo, Calif.: Dandy Lion Productions, 1985.

Zlotnick, Barbara Bradley. *Ready for Reference: Media Skills for Intermediate Students*. Littleton, Colo.: Libraries Unlimited, Inc., 1984.

Learning packages—library media specialist develops various activities, print or nonprint format, which are assigned to complete.

Advantage: appeal to a variety of modalities; can be designed to address specific skill objectives; activities can be expanded or interchanged.

Disadvantage: no immediate feedback; time consuming to prepare; can present a space problem.

For more information on learning packages see:

Jay, M. Ellen, and Hilda Jay. *Building Reference Skills in the Elementary School*. Hamden, Conn.: Library Professional Publications, 1986.

Magrabe, Mary. *The "Now" Library: A Station's Approach Media Center Teaching Kit*. Washington, D.C.: Acropolis Books, 1973.

Wehmeyer, Lillian Biermann. *The School Librarian as Educator*. 2nd ed. Littleton, Colo.: Libraries Unlimited, Inc., 1984.

Computer-aided instruction—students are instructed by using a computer software program.

Advantage: students enjoy using new technology; programs provide immediate feedback; commercially developed software is now available for different age groups.

Disadvantage: few library media centers have sufficient hardware to accommodate more than a few students at one time; commercial software rarely describes the local library media center accurately; good quality software is difficult to find.

For more information on computer-aided instruction see:

Gratch, Bonnie. "Computer-assisted Instruction: An Unfilled Promise." *Wilson Library Bulletin* 61 (December 1986): 20-22.

Trupiano, Rose. "CALICO: Teaching Library Skills to Students." *Computers in Libraries* 9 (February 1989): 27-29.

Lecture—live presentations made in preparation for an assignment or as part of general program.

Advantage: students are familiar with this approach; can reach a large number of students; presentation can be adapted to needs of group; allows for interaction.

Disadvantage: often seen as boring by students; students often become distracted if not properly motivated.

For more information on lectures see:

Fields, Carolyn B. "Using Results of a Pre-Test to Determine Lecture Content: A Case Study." *Research Strategies* 5 (Winter 1987): 29-35.

Kobelski, Pamela, and Mary Reichel. "Conceptual Frameworks for Bibliographic Instruction." *Journal of Academic Librarianship* 7 (May 1981): 73-74.

Peele, David. "The Hook Principle." *RQ* 13 (Winter 1973): 135-38.

Term paper clinic—through a formal conference with a library media specialist, students are individually helped to develop a search strategy for their library media center research.

Advantage: students have a specific need and are motivated; presentation is geared to individual level of knowledge; usually students see the results of the help and feel very positive about the library media center.

Disadvantage: very time consuming; difficult to schedule if a large number of students needs to be helped; students may allow library media specialists to do most of the thinking.

For more information on term paper clinics see:

Dubin, Eileen, Jitka Hurych, and Patricia McMillan. "An In-depth Analysis of a Term Paper Clinic." *Illinois Libraries* 60 (March 1978): 324-33.

Hughes, Phyllis, and Arthur Flandreau. "Tutorial Library Instruction: The Freshman Program at Berea College." *Journal of Academic Librarianship* 6 (1980): 91-94.

References to books and articles with complete program ideas:

American Library Association, Library Instruction Round Table Continuing Education Committee. *Case Studies in Library Instruction*, 1987.

Bell, Irene Wood, and Robert B. Brown. *Gaming in the Media Center Made Easy*. Littleton, Colo.: Libraries Unlimited, Inc., 1982.

Beyond Browsing: Library Media Skills—Kindergarten, Grades 1-8. Los Angeles, Calif.: Los Angeles Unified School District, 1980.

Dowell, Connie V. "Weaving Library Skills into the Curriculum." *RQ* 26 (Winter 1986): 165-67.

Glavich, Sister Mary Kirene. "The Boring and the Lively." *Learning Today* 12 (Summer/Fall 1979): 85-87.

A Guide to School Library Media Programs. Hartford, Conn.: Connecticut State Board of Education, 1982.

Hart, Thomas L., ed. *Instruction in School Media Center Use*. Chicago: American Library Association, 1978.

How-to-do-it: 22 Easy Lessons. Irvine, Calif.: Irvine Unified School District, 1980.

Instruction in Library Media Skills: Supplement to a Guide. Hartford, Conn.: Connecticut State Board of Education, 1984.

Irving, Ann. *Study and Information Skills across the Curriculum*. London: Heinemann Educational Books, 1985.

Jay, Hilda L. *Stimulating Student Search: Library Media/Classroom Teach Techniques*. Hamden, Conn.: Shoe String Press, 1983.

Kuhlthau, Carol Collier. *Teaching the Library Research Process: A Step-by-Step Program for Secondary School Students*. West Nyack, N.Y.: Center for Applied Research in Education, Inc., 1985.

Lewis, Z., comp. *Developing Learning Skills through Library Service, K-12*. Chicago: American Library Association, Library Instruction Round Table, 1981.

Magrabe, Mary. *Media Magic*. Washington, D.C.: Acropolis Books, 1980.

Magrabe, Mary. *The "Now" Library: A Station's Approach Media Center Teaching Kit*. Washington, D.C.: Acropolis Books, 1973.

Mallett, Jerry J. *Resource Rousers: Resource Book Usage*. West Nyack, N.Y.: Center for Applied Research in Education, Inc., 1982.

Media Ideas Handbook. Davenport, Iowa: Media Services Division, printed by Mississippi Bend AEA Media Center, 1980.

Nording, JoAnne. *Dear Faculty: A Discovery Method Guidebook to the High School Library*. Westwood, Mass.: F. W. Faxon, 1976.

Seaver, Alice R. *Library Media Skills: Strategies for Instructing Primary Students*. Littleton, Colo.: Libraries Unlimited, Inc., 1984.

Stacks of Ideas: Activities for Library Media Center and Classroom K-12. Oklahoma City, Okla.: Oklahoma State Department of Education, 1983.

Walker, H. Thomas, and Paula Kay Montgomery. *Teaching Media Skills: An Instructional Program for Elementary and Middle School Students*. 2nd ed. Littleton, Colo.: Libraries Unlimited, Inc., 1983.

Wehmeyer, Lillian Biermann. *The School Librarian as Educator*. 2nd ed. Littleton, Colo.: Libraries Unlimited, Inc., 1984.

Wisconsin Library Media Skills Guide. Madison, Wis.: Wisconsin School Library Media Association, 1979.

Library Program Skill Objectives:

A Guide to School Library Media Programs. Hartford, Conn.: Connecticut State Board of Education, 1982.

Hauschild, Ruth, and Bettye Wilson. *Library Skills Grades 3-8*. Wheeling, Ill.: Community Consolidated School District 21, 1982.

Study Skills: Study Your Way to Success, Kindergarten-6th. Norman, Okla.: Oklahoma State Department of Education, 1982.

STAFF AND FACILITY PLANNING

In order to maintain an effective information skills program, sufficient staff, space, and resources must be available. Elementary library media center staffs often have only one professional who, in turn, may or may not have paid clerical help. Junior and senior high schools often have more professional help available. Circumstances dictate the amount of budget, space, time, resources, and staff available to meet the information skills objectives.

Be realistic. Determine what you can handle without strain; more instructional services can be added as circumstances change. Overextending goals lead to patron disappointment with the program because of unkept promises. Needs can be met through a wide variety of approaches tailored to any budget, space, and staff. Some skills can be taught via indirect means—signs, posters, pathfinders, cassettes, or videotapes—other methods of learning will rely on interaction with staff. It is helpful to prepare a chart indicating what type of space, budget, staff, or equipment is involved to meet each given objective. This allows the library media specialist to view the options available and determine which are most viable. When obstacles of money or space are encountered, the library media specialist should seek support of the principal, district coordinator, PTA volunteers, or local businesses. Figure 4.1 is an example of a planning chart to delineate the objective—then brainstorm the requirements for every way you can think of to meet this objective.

For more information on staff assessment see:

Magrabe, Mary. *Media Magic*. Washington, D.C.: Acropolis Books, 1980, 44-47.

Martin, Betty, and Frances S. Hatfield. *The School District Library Media Director's Handbook*. Hamden, Conn.: Library Professional Publications, 1982.

Format	Staff	Time to Present	Space	Budget	Equipment
Booklet	Library Media Specialist Typist		Charge Desk Corner	$5 Printing and Paper	Typewriter and copier
Slide/Tape	Library Media Specialist or Classroom Teacher or Clerical Aide	½ hour	Classroom or Library	$15 Film and Cassette	Camera, Tape Recorder, Slide Projector
Lecture with Transparencies	Library Media Specialist	½ hour	Classroom or Library	$4.50 Markers and Transparency Film	Copier for Making Transparencies Overhead for Using Transparencies

Fig. 4.1. Example of a planning chart.

GAINING TEACHER COOPERATION

In the best academic environment, the teacher with an academic objective in mind that requires information skills discusses the assignment with the library media specialist. When the assignment requires media to teach the concept via a variety of modalities, a variety of sources are explored. When the instructional intent is to direct students to find their own concept sources, the methods for developing research strategies are the focus.

In the real world, this planning between teacher and library media specialist does not always occur. Many library media specialists learn of research assignments when faced with numerous students seeking assistance. What can be done to develop a close, cooperative relationship with the classroom teacher? The first and most important step is to ask yourself as a library media specialist whether you are willing to put the time and effort into pursuing this goal? Are you willing to put the paperwork of the library media center aside in order to spend time cultivating and communicating with the teaching staff of your school? If you are committed to getting the teachers into the library media center, here are some suggestions:

1. Get the teachers physically into the library media center by offering them something they want or need: free *New York Times*; food—morning coffee, afternoon cookies; a place to work—a study carrel, or computer.

2. Offer library media center services tailored to the faculty: interlibrary loans for faculty pursuing graduate work; Selective Dissemination of Information (SDI) service—send teachers citations, articles, or books on their personal or professional interests.

3. Communicate about library media center services: write to new teachers about library media center services; provide a newsletter to all teachers; prepare new booklists; issue memos on specific services as they become available.

4. Communicate about the library media center information skills program: share the program's objectives and outcomes via your faculty newsletter. Be sure to send the newsletter to superintendent and board members to keep them abreast of your program happenings.

5. Involve the library media center in the academic life of the school: join the curriculum committee; offer the library media center for faculty and department meetings; plan a program to be offered during parents' nights.

The point behind all of these efforts is very simple—as the teachers become more familiar with the library media center and its resources, they will come to understand the positive impact it can make on the educational program. Once they understand the full potential of the library media center program for their students, they will be more willing to incorporate the library media center instructional program into their academic units.

For more information on gaining teacher cooperation see:

Didier, Elaine K. "An Overview of Research on the Impact of School Library Media Programs on Student Achievement." *School Library Media Quarterly* 14 (Fall 1985): 33-36.

Haycock, Carol-Ann. "Information Skills in the Curriculum: Developing a School-Based Continuum." *Emergency Librarian* 13 (September/October 1985): 11-17.

Huber, Kris, and Patricia Lewis. "Tired of Term Papers? Options for Librarians and Professors." *Research Strategies* 2 (Fall 1984): 192-99.

Junior High School Library/Media Skills. Lancaster, Pa.: School District of Lancaster, Pennsylvania, September 1983.

Magrabe, Mary. *Media Magic.* Washington, D.C.: Acropolis Books, 1980, 1-23.

O'Hanlon, Nancyanne. "Up the Down Staircase: Establishing Library Instruction for Teachers." *RQ* 27 (Summer 1988): 528-33.

EVALUATION

Most library media specialists understand the term evaluation to mean measuring the impact the instruction program has had. Thomas Kirk states that instruction evaluation is a systematic collection of data to determine as precisely as possible the cause-and-effect relationships among student backgrounds, bibliographic instruction programs, library media center use, and student attitudes towards the library media center.

Clearly, evaluation permits the library media specialist to determine if the program objectives have been met. It is, however, not the end of the process of program planning; it is a critical part of ongoing program development, since it guides future planning.

When the evaluation shows that the program objectives are being met, the library media specialist can use this information to show teachers and administrators the value of the instruction program, thus gaining much needed support for the library media center. When, on the other hand, the evaluation shows the program falls short of desired results, the library media specialist has the information needed to adjust the program so it will be more successful in the future.

It is difficult to evaluate a program because there are many factors which contribute to an information skills program. It is important to identify these factors before an evaluation instrument is designed. Are you trying to evaluate the library media specialist as an effective teacher, the program goals, the instructional method, or the level of student ability? What is to be measured will dictate the evaluation process. For example, if the library media specialist is to be evaluated, the method might be peer observation, informal student feedback, or a brief teacher/student questionnaire. If, on the other hand, the program's impact on student knowledge about the library media center is to be measured, a pre- and post-test, graded exercises, or bibliography study might be used.

Preparing the evaluation instrument is almost as difficult as preparing the program. For the evaluation instrument to be accurate, the design must ensure validity and reliability. Validity means that it measures what you think it does, while reliability means that it measures the same way all the time.

Program evaluation design should not be left until the end. Judging the effectiveness of an instruction program is a logical component of the whole process of developing the program's objectives. In other words, as an objective is agreed upon, the instructional methods and the method of evaluation should be described. For example, if the objective of the lesson is to teach students how to use *The Readers' Guide*, the evaluation procedure could be to see if, given a topic, the student can identify and translate an appropriate citation. Care should be taken not to include locating the periodical article unless that has also been made an objective, because that is a separate skill.

What follows are some examples of evaluation methods which may prove useful to the school library media specialist.

Informal Evaluation Methods

Feedback during instruction—library media specialist observes students to gauge their attentiveness, and the questions they ask and answer.

Advantage: the library media specialist can immediately adjust to students' reactions.

Disadvantage: it is difficult to make dramatic adjustments in a presentation once it is under way.

Student/faculty interviews—library media specialist can ask student/faculty member about the presentation and receive suggestions following a presentation.

Advantage: students/faculty may offer positive suggestions in a relaxed atmosphere which doesn't require anything more than an impromptu response.

Disadvantage: the reactions are not likely to be analytical or particularly critical. It is difficult for individuals to express negative reactions in a one-to-one situation.

Observing students using the library media center—library media specialist can observe the class using the library media center following the presentation.

Advantage: student behavior will indicate the impact of the instruction.

Disadvantage: the library media specialist can only observe a few students at one time, and the library media specialist may not really be very objective.

Formal Evaluation Methods

Library media center exercises—students are required to follow-up instruction with written work.

Advantage: the exercise can actually reinforce the learning, while indicating what has been learned. The exercise, if graded, may actually motivate students to pay more attention to instruction.

Disadvantage: exercises take time to design and grade. If there are a large number of students, exercises often turn into group projects rather than an individual effort.

Research journals—students are asked to record the subject headings, books, and periodicals identified for their research topic.

Advantage: simulates actual library media center use.

Disadvantage: topics will be supported by different resources; time consuming and difficult to grade.

Post-test—students are given an objective test.

Advantage: this format quickly indicates what students have retained from presentation.

Disadvantage: does not simulate real library media center use situation; takes valuable class time.

Questionnaires to students or faculty—students or faculty are surveyed to learn their reactions to the presentation.

Advantage: allows the users to express themselves about the instructional program.

Disadvantage: time consuming to design a questionnaire which is reliable and valid; students do not always take questionnaires seriously; it is not always easy to collect the questionnaires from the faculty.

Videotaped presentation—the presentation is taped as it is given.

Advantage: library media specialists can see themselves in class as others see them.

Disadvantage: the library media specialist and/or the students may find it unnerving and unnatural to be taped.

For more information on evaluation see:

Adams, Mignon. "Effects of Evaluation on Teaching Methods." In *Improving Library Instruction: How to Teach and How to Evaluate*, edited by Carolyn A. Kirkendall. Ann Arbor, Mich.: Pierian Press, 1979.

Fatzer, Jill B. "Evaluation of Library User Instruction." *RQ* 27 (Fall 1987): 41-43.

For more information on annual program evaluation see:

Davies, Ruth Ann. *The School Library Media Center: A Force for Educational Excellence*. 2nd ed. New York: R. R. Bowker Company, 1974, 259-77.

Procedures Manual for School Library Media Centers. Oklahoma City, Okla.: Oklahoma State Department of Education, 1982, 155-74.

Wehmeyer, Lillian Biermann. *The School Librarian as Educator*. 2nd ed. Littleton, Colo.: Libraries Unlimited, Inc., 1984.

Yesner, B. L., and H. L. Jay. *The School Administrator's Guide to Evaluating Library Media Programs*. Hamden, Conn.: Shoe String Press, 1987.

PART V
SPECIAL LIBRARIES

Planning for Library Instruction in Special Libraries

Tobeylynn Birch
Director of the Library
California School of
Professional Psychology
Los Angeles, California

Emily Bergman
Assistant Librarian
California School of
Professional Psychology
Los Angeles, California

Susan J. Arrington
Head of Government
Reference Service
State Library Resource Center
Enoch Pratt Free Library
Baltimore, Maryland

Whether or not the term library instruction, bibliographic instruction, or user education is used, the teaching process is important in special libraries and is often done without being labeled as such. Because special libraries are often staffed by only one or two overworked individuals, user education is frequently undertaken with little advance planning; signs are posted if more than a few users ask the same directional questions, and tours are provided upon request by administrators or new employees.

This reactive approach does not create the type of integrated, systematic program that can easily be evaluated for efficacy and revised to meet changing needs. Any user education program, regardless of its extent, should not be implemented without adequate planning and preparation as described in this handbook. The process of setting up a library instruction program from inception to actual implementation will take some time, possibly nine to twelve months for the entire process. Although the time for planning may not seem available, the planning process will save time in the long run.

Special libraries present a unique situation and opportunity for library instruction. Many special libraries have two types of patrons—those who work for or are members of the parent organization and use the library in the course of their work, and those who work outside the organization and use the library for a variety of reasons. Educating each type is an entirely different experience, each with its own set of goals, objectives, and formats. Although some special libraries have only in-house patrons, who are more identifiable and predictable, library instruction programs for both type of patrons will be addressed.

TYPES OF SPECIAL LIBRARIES

Special libraries can be grouped by the types of organizations they serve, including corporate, law, medical, government, private research, cultural, religious (e.g., church), nonprofit (e.g., association or society), and special subject (i.e., within a larger library). The in-house patrons they serve can include permanent employees, both clerical and professional;

consultants or adjunct employees, such as visiting professors; part-time employees; and temporary employees, such as seasonal workers, summer interns, and special project employees. Patrons external to the organization may be sporadic or one-time users, or they may need to use the library regularly. For example, urban planning students might frequent a regional planning library, or importers might use the U.S. Customs Service Library or the U.S. International Trade Commission Library. Each library's discrete user groups must be identified and considered because they will have differing library instruction needs and requirements and the library will need to decide how to handle each group and in what situations. The instruction may not be with the end user but with support staff, such as secretaries or research assistants.

In addition to types of organizations and patrons served, the types of materials held will need to be considered in planning an instruction program. Like most libraries, special libraries will probably contain books and journals. However, they may also contain many other types of publications and media: microforms; audiovisual materials, such as films, videocassettes, tapes, records, slides, filmstrips, and slide/tape presentations; government documents and technical reports; online systems; picture collections; unique indexes, whether paper or automatic; rare books or archival materials; and newspapers. The extent of the collection in each of these areas and the amount and nature of use of each format should influence the structure and content of user education. For example, instruction in the use of audiovisual materials may include instruction on how to operate the machinery involved, which would require an appropriate setting as well as instructional design.

BENEFITS OF A LIBRARY INSTRUCTION PROGRAM

Justifying a library instruction program in a special library, where end users may expect the librarian to provide the answers, is much more difficult than in school and academic libraries, where library instruction is seen as an extension of the educational process. However, a library instruction program can benefit everyone involved—individual users, the parent organization, and the library itself. As employees learn to access library resources previously unknown to them, their performance will improve, they will be able to use their time more efficiently and find better information to support their work. For example, a lawyer can save valuable time searching for a precedent by learning to use LEXIS more efficiently, an engineer can save time not having to redraw a design that already exists by learning to use or ask for the appropriate resources, or a scientist can avoid duplicating research by learning where to look for this kind of information. As users learn more about the library, they will also use library staff more effectively, asking more appropriate and more intelligent questions. All of this can save money for the whole organization and even contribute to profits. After all, successful decisions depend on individuals learning how to find the best information, not just the easiest.

Library instruction may also have a positive effect on the budget. Educating employees about the availability of information in the library will encourage them to use its central resources instead of creating or adding to scattered office collections. Over time, better use of the library's collection will reduce resource duplication in various locations, resulting in cost savings to the organization. More money may then be available to the library, particularly if office materials are purchased with library funds.

Library instruction can also be an effective public relations tool. In some cases, use of the library may be the only contact the public has with the organization. Helping these patrons make better use of the library and showing concern for their needs will reflect well on the organization. Internal relations may also improve with the program and garner much needed support for the library. The librarian can enhance his or her importance as an information officer by demonstrating the difference between an information person and a storage and retrieval person. A library instruction program that is integrated into the workings of the organization can help the librarian make the necessary connections to become an indispensable influence on the decision-making process.

Finally, better use of resources may create demand for more resources. As employees learn more about what is available, they often generate more requests for both interlibrary loans and new purchases. Heavy demand, evidenced by these requests, can justify increased budgets for library materials. In addition, analysis of interlibrary loan requests can aid in the formulation or strengthening of a selection policy for the library.

NEEDS ASSESSMENT

Before a user education program can be planned, the clients who will be served and their needs must be identified. This can be accomplished by several distinct but not exclusive methods: observation, data collection, and surveys. These strategies may be conducted concurrently, which would save time. On the other hand, the more formal methods of needs assessment would be more effective if based on information uncovered by an initial informal assessment. However

accomplished, the assessment should consider the whole organization, not just the library and its users and potential users.

Observation

All library staff in a position to observe patrons' use of the library should be asked to contribute their perceptions about reference transactions, interlibrary loan patterns, and collection development practices. In particular, note reference questions that are asked frequently and which groups of users ask them. Observation may also help to identify particular cycles of questions or requests that correspond to predictable cycles within or external to the parent organization. For example, a library serving an accounting firm is likely to receive more questions about tax laws during the early months of the year. Such patterns can help determine when instruction should be scheduled. Allow enough time for the process of observation to include at least one cycle and several if possible.

Data Collection

Along with observation, keep detailed statistics or numbers and types of reference transactions, patrons, and interlibrary loan requests. This process may seem tedious, but the quantitative data can be particularly important when justifying budget requests or convincing the administration to support the proposed instruction program.

Survey

Do not stop with the staff's observations and statistical data. If a program is based solely on what the library has determined is necessary, it may not appeal to the users and therefore will fail. Any planning time must take into consideration what the users desire and how they perceive their needs. This information can be gathered in several ways.

First, informally talk with patrons in the library, including both in-house and outside users. Use other settings as well, such as staff meetings, to informally survey within the organization. Ask users in what ways they use the library and what would help them use it better, and ask nonusers why they do not use the library. Schedule meetings with users and library staff to brainstorm about possible instruction.

Second, develop a formal survey to be distributed to all potential users. If possible, solicit help from other departments of the parent organization in designing the survey. For example, a research and development department or a marketing department may have individuals with expertise in designing such instruments. Other libraries may also be able to help by providing samples of needs assessments they have done. Keep the survey short and to the point, beginning with a sentence or two of background and explanation as to why the information is important. If the term instruction would be meaningless to users and would not yield useful information, include a brief definition of instruction. Multiple choice questions may result in a higher response rate because they are quicker to fill out; however, open-ended questions can encourage more detailed responses.

The content of the survey should include such questions as:

- How and why the respondents currently use the library.

- What kind of instruction they now receive.

- What additional instruction or guidance they could use.

- What aspects of their jobs would be enhanced by increased knowledge and use of the library.

- How much time they have for instruction.

- What forum and when is most suitable for them.

Surveys should be distributed through several channels to reach the most potential users. Giving them to patrons as they use the library may be the easiest, but this will not reach infrequent patrons and nonusers. Be more systematic and send the surveys to department or division heads for distribution to all employees. If feasible, address and mail the survey to each person individually. Patrons from outside the organization can be reached by mail if a log of their names and addresses has been kept. For the most part, only current public patrons or those who have used the library in the past will be surveyed. Be sure to include a date by which the response is due, and make the survey easy to return, perhaps including a return envelope.

When all the observations, data collection, and surveys are completed, tabulate and analyze the information objectively. The needs assessment will make clear which groups want or need library instruction and help indicate the priority each group should receive, based on its particular needs. Establishing instruction priorities can be rather complex, because they are based on institutional as well as library goals, fundamental as well as more specialized learning needs, and primary as well as influential users. The library must consider the importance of groups within the organization. A group that does not show as much interest on the needs assessment may actually take priority based on the organizational hierarchy. Consider the political aspects as well, such as a group that provides financial or influential support to the library. Finally, the primary or heavy users may actually be the most knowledgeable about the library, but at the same time take priority because of their relationship with the library. Consider the same priorities for outside patrons as well as in-house patrons. The only juggling problem may be in finding time to accommodate both. Concentrating on a few programs will succeed better than spreading efforts over many. (See pp. 98-105 for examples of user surveys in libraries having special needs.)

IDENTIFYING POTENTIAL PROGRAMS

Concurrent with the needs assessment, gather information on the types of instruction that could be offered. Begin by identifying what instruction is currently provided. Librarians already offer many library instruction services such as printed signs, help at the card catalog, advice on computer sources,

and point-of-use explanations for particular reference tools. Evaluate how these help or hinder the user and how they might be incorporated into a larger, more systematic program.

Decide what are the functions of the library, such as online searching, reference, notifying users of the latest findings on their topics, and even public relations, collection development, and cataloging. Decide which functions can be enhanced by a user education program, and ignore, for the time being, those that do not have an instruction component. For example, if computer searching and routing information on the latest findings are the functions identified for user education, then they become the main focus for the development of a program. On the other hand, if the library is primarily a book collection where historical significance is of value, the program would focus on successful use of the catalog and key reference sources. The library functions that have led to the instruction program will also help the librarian decide how to attack the instruction, such as by in-service training, written materials, or one-on-one instruction.

List any requests for service that could not be met due to lack of time, opportunity, or resources. These may include requests for instruction on an online service or a detailed explanation of how certain materials interrelate or can be used in conjunction with each other. Then list services that should be offered, given unlimited staff, time, and resources. Consider all the possibilities, including those suggested by library staff and patrons.

Next, gather information on library instruction by reviewing the literature and consulting colleagues. A bibliography is included in this handbook. In addition, a search in ERIC, LISA, and *Library Literature* (either print or electronic indexes) will turn up quite a bit of literature on library instruction. Do not be discouraged that very little of it deals specifically with special libraries. Most ideas on library instruction are transferrable; with a little imagination, many can be adapted quite well to another library's situation. Check the management literature on training and development. It too can be adapted for any special library user group, from college students to corporate executives.

Colleagues in similar libraries may be able to provide suggestions. The local chapter of the Special Libraries Association or the local or state library association can supply names of librarians who have developed instruction programs. A clearinghouse of library instruction information may exist locally, as well as in the state and nationally. The state library may provide advisory or support services. The training and development or human resources department in the parent organization may be able to provide ideas or support. And, consultants can be helpful, if budgetary support is available. Once again, do not discount programs from other types of libraries. If they have some similarities in patron usage, staff size, or resources, they could be very helpful.

GOALS

When all the information has been gathered and analyzed, goals for the program can be developed. A goal is a broad philosophical statement of an ongoing mission. Goals are used to determine the aim of a program and to tell when its purpose has been achieved. Using the results of the needs assessment, involve the entire library staff in the formulation of goals. Make sure to align the goals with both the library's and the parent organization's short- and long-range goals, ensuring the instruction program an integral role in the library's service and the organization's mission. Some general examples of how the goals might read are as follows:

- To raise the level of library skills in the organization.

- To increase the knowledge of available library services.

- To increase the number of library users among new employees.

OBJECTIVES

Once goals are developed, write objectives for them. Objectives should contain concrete results to be achieved within a specific time. Make sure objectives are formulated so they may be measured for evaluation. A program is considered successful if it has met its objectives.

example: All lawyers and paralegals in the organization will be trained on LEXIS within one year.

Allow enough time to accomplish the objectives, taking into consideration budget and resources, and make the project appropriate to the population served and to the goal to be met.

For each objective, write strategies to explain how the objective will be accomplished. Strategies are action-oriented and taken together will create a workplan and a timetable. Put intermediary time frames on the strategies so progress can be monitored. In keeping with the objective example above, some sample strategies may be as follows:

1. In the first month, identify participants to be trained.

2. By the second month, determine optimum number of participants per session, design instruction, and set the total number of training classes needed.

3. During the next two months, schedule and carry out number of classes needed.

4. By the sixth month, evaluate training sessions and tabulate results.

5. In the seventh month, hold follow-up interviews with participants.

6. In the eighth month, hold follow-up sessions as indicated by interviews.

7. By the tenth month, create a mechanism to automatically train new employees.

WORKING WITH THE ADMINISTRATION

As with any new project, the organization's administration should be involved in the implementation of a library instruction program. Depending on the library's position in the organization and the extent of the proposed program, administrative approval may be required early in the planning process. Secure financial support if the program will require additional budget, and clear the use of personnel and other resources with the organizational hierarchy. Even if approval is not required for minor changes in the budget or functions of the library, maintaining communication with administration will garner support for the program.

Gaining administrative support can be anything from easy to extremely difficult, depending on a number of factors: the librarian's position in the organization, the working relationship with his or her supervisor, the size of the project, and the resources needed to accomplish it. If the needs assessment provides a strong justification, goals and objectives are written clearly to meet those needs, and all the facts and figures back the proposal, the program should seem reasonable to the administration. Additional written and verbal support from library patrons will be invaluable in gaining support from the administration.

If the administration will not approve additional funds or resources, the program may need to be modified or scaled back. Be prepared to present several options, ranging from the most comprehensive to the minimum that is acceptable. Most administrations will at least be willing to venture with the least expensive option. If such a pilot program proves successful, support may then be forthcoming for an expanded program.

STAFF RESOURCES

Choosing which staff members to be involved will be influenced by the extent of the training to be undertaken. In addition to the actual instruction or preparation of materials, someone will need to administer the program. In small libraries, all functions may be handled by the same person; larger libraries may include an entire training staff with its own administrator. Have several planning sessions with the staff and try to get all of them involved to the fullest extent possible, regardless of who will do the training. This allows everyone to have input in the new program and to be supportive of the training team when it is formed. Assess the talents of each staff member and try to match interests and abilities with the tasks at hand. Make sure everyone understands exactly what he or she is supposed to do, and put all instructions in writing.

Recognize that if staff already have a full load of responsibilities they will need release time to plan, implement, and evaluate the program. Duties will need to be shifted somewhat to accommodate instructional responsibilities. Consider staff development and training for everyone involved in the planning and presentation of the instruction. Librarians and other staff may need to learn how to teach, including not only teaching skills and tips, but also how to be interesting, whether in oral presentations or written materials.

Take advantage of team building, which involves more staff and spreads out the responsibility and time used. Allow two or three people to share a program, and that program becomes more well rounded with a complement of strengths and weaknesses. This works especially well with a novice and a seasoned veteran as a team, which along with the aforementioned training will help bring new or reluctant staff into the program.

Involve everyone in the library with whom users come in contact as part of the program. This has a two-sided advantage. First, staff support is more assured if everyone feels part of the new program and has a chance to help make the project work with suggestions and observations. Second, users will become more familiar with certain individuals and will know to whom to come for help. For example, have the person responsible for interlibrary loans involved in the part of the program about interlibrary loans, the circulation staff involved concerning circulation procedures, or the online searcher involved about databases.

Once available staff are assigned to all the tasks, further assistance may be required. Where possible, use staff from other departments with the organization, for example, secretaries or clerks for help in typing or filing, graphic artists for signs and posters, or the public relations officer for publicity in and outside of the organization at the right time. If an organizational database is located in the library and is part of the instruction program, employ someone from the division that created the database to assist in the training. Explore becoming an integral part of the orientation program for new employees, if your organization has one.

If staff are not available or the expertise does not exist within the organization, outside consultants can be used for parts of the program, or you may decide to contract out the entire training program. Consultants can be librarians, vendors, academics, or specialists who are involved in training as a profession. They may be used to set up a program; work on improving an existing program; teach a single session of a multisession course; demonstrate a particular product, such as an online system; or teach an entire course. Contracting with a consultant, of course, takes money, but if you can show it is the most cost-effective way to meet the goal, it is worth pursuing. Consultants can be found through resource lists, such as a speakers' bureau, recommendations from colleagues, or directories, such as the *Consultants and Consulting Organizations Directory*.

MATERIAL RESOURCES

The material resources may also be found internally or external to the organization. Teaching materials can cover a wide range of items. Most materials can be prepared in-house, but also look at packaged programs if they exist for your purposes. These may involve some cost, so keep that in mind for budget justification. If you intend to use audiovisuals, allow time to have them produced and make sure the appropriate equipment for their use is available. Cost may also be a factor for audiovisuals, especially if they have to be commercially produced because in-house facilities do not exist, or if the in-house facility must charge them against the library's budget.

When teaching the use of particular research tools, obtain extra copies of such items for classroom use; this cost too should be figured into the budget and time allowed for acquisition. Check whether the library will be charged for classroom space or equipment use by other departments. When teaching use of vendor-produced items such as online databases, check into obtaining free instructional-use time and brochures.

In planning the format of the program, keep in mind the setting needed. Do not plan for very large groups if no classrooms or auditoriums exist in the organization. When using a videotape or slide/tape program for groups, a darkened room must be available. Consider a road-show program—taking the program to the users' site rather than having them come to the library—if space in the library is a problem or if you are trying to reach outside users. For library tours and orientations, be sure the library is laid out such that the group will not be crowded or get lost. Library instruction also requires work and storage space, which needs to be planned along with the instruction. Space and equipment requirements are listed in the "Modes of bibliographic instruction" table in the overview chapter (pp. 10-13); know the possibilities and limitations of the library's environment when reviewing these teaching methods.

SCHEDULING

In planning instruction, be very careful of scheduling. Choose times that are convenient for the users, not the library. Although this may seem obvious at the outset, some groups may require night or weekend instruction, especially outside patrons. A particular shift in a hospital may need very early or late programs, whereas a church group may need only weekend programs; a corporate or law library program will most likely take place during business hours, but scheduling may require sensitivity to daily routine. Although a lunchtime seminar program may be very effective, avoid scheduling anything right after lunch when people become sleepy in a sit-and-listen situation, or program more active sessions where people are able to move around and participate. Be aware of the problem of stragglers if scheduling sessions first thing in the morning. When using a workbook, schedule a time for it to be distributed as well as returned. That schedule may determine the format of the workbook itself.

INSTRUCTIONAL DESIGN

The method of instruction chosen for the program should be designed with its specific audience and objectives in mind. Be sure the instructional design is appropriate to the expertise of the population. For example, an introduction to the computer may seem too elementary for research scientists, whereas computer-aided instruction may be threatening to a church group. Use appropriate technology and media whenever possible, and in selecting a mode of instruction, consider the following factors: users' short-term and long-term needs, depth of instruction required to meet informational needs, amount of time available for participation, effectiveness of mode in terms of retention, preparation time required, available personnel, and ease of revision of materials.

MODES OF INSTRUCTION

Library tours and orientation sessions are the most common types of library orientation/instruction and get much of the instruction message across without much cost and without threatening users. In planning a new program, starting an orientation program with new employees or public users will be easiest. New accountants in a CPA firm, for example, will be eager to learn about library services, whereas the partners may want nothing to do with the library.

Exhibits and signs should be used creatively with user education in mind. They do not require the continued involvement of the librarian and are always available. The most helpful point-of-use printed aids are succinct and clear. Two concerns when producing this kind of instructional aid are the message to be conveyed and the shortest way to relay it. Do not crowd information into every inch of space available, or the user will think there is too much to learn. A multipage exhibit, such as a flip chart, will give a few simple instructions per page, and each page will remain uncluttered. To retain simplicity, break instructions into straightforward statements or sections, avoiding paragraphs or even sentences. Even directional signs must be absolutely clear; sometimes a label with an arrow is more confusing than no sign at all. Make all signage systematic so it all ties together. Thinking of signage as part of the instruction program and not just a collection of signs will help make them more meaningful. Avoid handwritten signs and always use good graphics and design. Test all point-of-use aids, signs, and directions before making them permanent.

One-on-one instruction may be the most time-consuming method, but the user can get exactly the information he or she needs at the time it is needed, which makes the retention of the information more likely. The line between this kind of instruction and answering reference questions may be a fine one, but teaching a user how to use the card catalog, including the use of subject headings and added entries on catalog cards, instead of merely retrieving a particular book or piece of information, should be considered part of instruction. After all, the next time the user needs information, he or she may be able to find it independently, and that is the reward of teaching.

Videotapes and slide/tape programs have been proven effective but may be too costly, both in terms of financial support and the time and expertise involved in production. Revision is difficult when sources change or become outdated. However, these programs can be in more than one place at a time and used repeatedly by patrons at their convenience. Decide whether they are to be used in a workshop format or as point-of-use instruction.

Computer-aided instruction is becoming more common, but besides the equipment and programming costs involved, the instruction is often not portable, and teaching users how to use the program may make this mode impractical. When planning computer software for library instruction, you must learn how to use screen space, computer logic, and memory to teach; provide for competencies in a computer language;

design the program; program the material that has been scripted; write documentation; make copies for use; and package the documentation with the program. A few commercial programs are available.

Handouts, whether bibliographies or workbooks, provide a product that can be taken from the library and that users can refer to after instruction. Use both sides of the page so that written materials are not used as scrap paper. Try to design self-paced workbooks with exciting visuals that will keep the user's interest.

If a workshop or classroom lecture format is possible, this is often the most economical use of the librarian's time and can be the most thorough method to get across information. Do not try to cover every possible way the library might be used; information overload will decrease retention. Limiting the subject matter to a single focus is optimum. In outlining the lecture, follow the logical research procedure the users should follow, though this may not be how they actually do research, especially prior to library instruction. Examples of integrated workshop programs are the in-service or continuing education credit classes given in a medical library or information sessions held at a government lab whenever a new database is available so that employees know the very latest sources for the information they need.

If available, a parent organization's internal newsletter or staff publication provides an opportunity for general instruction. A library column can be used to describe how to use sources. General kinds of sources can be described, such as indexes or annual reviews, or use of specific tools can be explained. This is an especially good way to bring new resources, databases, or procedures to the attention of a wide audience of users. The role of the library and librarian is not only a good topic for public relations, but can help create more efficient use of the library.

PROGRAM DELIVERY

Incorporate program delivery methods that are most beneficial to the participants. Within any program, demonstrate skills and display materials. Use the book, journal, media, or computer itself, and be absolutely explicit in how to use it as well as where it fits within a search strategy. Whenever possible, allow hands-on experience: pass books around the room at a lecture, or require the user to find particular information by using all the relevant parts of a handbook. In workshops or orientations, consider an interactive learning mode by drawing on users' experience and questions while presenting the program. Keep written materials short to avoid boredom or overwhelming the user with too much information. For example, several one-page bibliographies or pathfinders on different subjects will be used more than one lengthy listing, even if it is divided by subject. Remember that if information cannot be easily located, it is unlikely to be used.

When preparing or pretesting material for a lecture or workshop, use peers of the target population if possible. For example, work with a lawyer on a LEXIS program or an account executive on a program explaining the use of advertising reference works. Not only are people outside the library brought into cooperation with the library, but the library can benefit from the expertise of those who will be actually using the information. Using peers may also increase acceptance of the instructional program and contribute to enhanced respect for and recognition of the librarians.

PROGRAM CONTENT

Keep the content of the program specific to the needs of the population. The needs assessment can identify what to teach. Do not teach *Readers' Guide* to medical students or the techniques of computer searching if the librarian always serves as the intermediary anyway. If the library's role within the organization is to provide all secondary research, teach what is available without the actual techniques of using the library resources. Only information that will be used will be remembered, and trying to cover all possible needs will not help the users if those needs are not immediate. The two most important points to stress in any instruction program using any media are the role of the librarian in the research process and search strategy. If users know how to formulate an effective method for research and how the librarian can help them, they will be more intelligent users of the research materials, even if they do not remember the specifics.

As librarians become increasingly involved in automation, the need for more library instruction becomes evident. Users need to know that databases exist that can provide the needed information, even if they do not do their own searching, and they should be alerted as soon as new databases become available. Online catalogs also necessitate instruction. Consider more than one mode of instruction, such as point-of-use instruction at the terminal and classes for users. As newer techniques are brought in, such as laser-disks and CD-ROM, prepare users for what they can and cannot do and how to use the hardware and software.

As users do more searching on automated systems themselves, teaching search strategy to end-users is a more efficient use of library staff time than working with each individual searcher on each individual search. In teaching end-users to search databases, include not only instruction in the formulation of search strategy and accessing the databases, but also provide time and hardware for hands-on practice.

PUBLICITY

Any instructional program requires publicity to get off the ground. Reach people with signs and flyers where they work, not just in the library. Use existing communication vehicles, such as an organizational newsletter, interoffice mail, or electronic mail. Similar outside media are effective in reaching the public as well, especially trade newsletters and electronic mail. Word-of-mouth publicity is often the most persuasive; library supporters and users have contacts with their peers and should be used. Solicit supervisors to encourage their workers to participate. Use refreshments as a drawing card; food can make the prospect of a "class" more palatable for many.

EVALUATION

When evaluating instruction programs, using involved pretest/post-test evaluations is recommended by some, but in most special libraries this is rarely feasible due to lack of time and staff. Nevertheless, evaluation is essential to improve the program, to retain administrative support, and to measure attainment of objectives.

Three types of evaluation are both useful and plausible. First, use a written evaluation. If a formal survey with experimental and control groups is feasible, one can determine what segments of the program work or do not work. Help with the formal evaluation may be found among colleagues within the organization or, again, by using a consultant. When a written survey is drawn up to evaluate instruction, it should be tested by nonlibrarians first to see if it makes sense. Keep the form very short, preferably on only one side of a page. Make the questions quick to answer, at the same time leaving room for comments. Collect the evaluations immediately after the program, while it is still fresh in the minds of the participants. If they are permitted to return the evaluations after leaving the site of the program, the evaluations are as likely to be tossed or forgotten as returned. Second, ask for and listen to verbal responses to the program. Participants are likely to express their problems or satisfaction with what they have learned when they are next confronted with using the library tool they were taught. Third, observe library use. Although a written evaluation is critical for a program involving lectures, audiovisuals, and handbooks, it is nearly impossible for point-of-use and certain written instructional materials, such as bibliographies. Nevertheless, by listening to users and by watching library use, evaluations of the instruction's effectiveness can still be gleaned. Note whether users can use the library more easily and whether reference questions indicate that they have understood the instruction. For example, a librarian knows a videotape on online searching needs revision if users who have viewed the tape are still confused about basic elements of searching.

If the evaluation shows that the program needs improvement, work backwards to determine the problem. The following checklist can begin the process. The "yes" and "no" answers will show where the program needs attention.

1. Is the mode of instruction appropriate to the:

   A. information?

   B. environment?

   C. intended audience?

2. Did the program include:

   A. too much information?

   B. too little information?

   C. content that is too difficult?

   D. content that is too simplistic?

   E. information inappropriate for current use?

3. Did people not attend the sessions or use the instructional materials because of:

    A. poor scheduling?

    B. poor physical placement or environment?

    C. miscommunications?

4. Was the staff:

    A. adequate in number?

    B. appropriately trained?

    C. interested and enthusiastic?

5. Is the organization's support adequate with:

    A. time?

    B. money?

    C. interest and enthusiasm?

6. Does the program meet the objectives?

7. Do the objectives and the program meet the goals?

8. Are the goals and objectives reasonable or appropriate in relation to the needs assessment?

CONCLUSION

Special libraries are extremely diverse, serving various patrons, organizations, and purposes. However, information programs can be of benefit to any special library by educating the organization's employees to make more and better use of the library's resources. Library procedures will be enhanced by instruction as users learn how to formulate their information search, what information is available, and how to access it most thoroughly, systematically, and easily. Library instruction rarely cuts down on librarians' work; on the contrary, it often increases. However, the librarians' time is better spent if users know how to formulate their questions and can independently do their more basic research themselves. More sophisticated and efficient use of library resources reflects well on the special library staff and should yield practical benefits for the parent organization.

APPENDIX: TWO CASE STUDIES OF THE IMPACT OF LIBRARY INSTRUCTION PLANNING

Two different kinds of special libraries and the planning and implementation of their library instruction programs are described. Neither the organizations nor the programs actually exist but are patterned after libraries known to the authors. The planning is simplified; the goals and objectives, in particular, are not as in-depth as they could be, and many possibilities exist for programming, but had to be planned within the limitations of time, money, and personnel. The planning, decisions, and programs impact each other and the organization, and show how to put the theory into practice.

TLC Advertising Agency

Type of Library

This is a corporate library with only in-house patrons. In the organization, it is part of the research department. The librarians do almost all the secondary research for employees using their own library as well as other collections in the city, such as the public library and the local university library. The two librarians try to anticipate questions by providing a sort of selective dissemination of information (SDI) program, sending appropriate articles, particularly to the account executives, from the periodicals held by the library. The collection is predominantly a journal collection with small reference and circulating collections related to advertising, the clients' products, or general information. A large picture file as well as a vertical file are organized by subject, and in-house reports are housed in the library as well. The library has access to the major database vendors. Two clerks handle circulation, serials control, filing, copying, and other clerical duties.

Description of Advertising Organization

An account executive (AE) is responsible for the business side of an account, or client. Each account has at least one AE and big ones may have more. A vice-president is responsible for the account department. The words of an advertisement are written by the copywriter and the picture, regardless of type of media, is the responsibility of the art director. Copywriters and art directors may work on more than one account at a time; they make up the creative department. Each account is a single product or advertising campaign. One company may have several products, but each is treated as an individual account.

Benefits of a Library Instruction Program

The librarians saw three specific benefits of a library instruction program. First, the employees would do better work and make more informed decisions because they will get better information more easily. Second, the library would become more visible and the librarians would receive more respect, raising the possibility of a higher library budget and salaries. Third, employees would become more effective library users by asking more precise questions and using well-planned search strategies.

Needs Assessment

The librarians observed library use, particularly the kinds of questions asked. Notes were made: what the general subjects were, how easily queries were answered, how the information was found, what department the questions came from, how long the turnaround time was, and what the information was needed for, if known. The librarians learned that account executives repeatedly asked for certain ready-reference, company and market research data that could require quite a bit of time, both in personnel and online use, to pull together. For example, the account executive on a petroleum account needed to know the latest information on alternative sources of energy, including how much is being used, who is producing it, who is using it, where the money is coming from, what research is being done, and government involvement in research, subsidies, and tax breaks. Market information for a lawn mower account might include a question like how many lawns are in the United States. The creative department needed pictures, general information, and answers to trivia questions for a soda pop advertisement, such as how much soda pop would fill the Statue of Liberty. The research department was particularly interested in forecasting and methodology information. The media department rarely used the library; all their reference books were in their department, so their only questions were usually ready-reference, company information.

In preparing the formal survey, the librarians got help from the research department. The researchers' expertise in primary research helped to create a short questionnaire that managed to elicit the information the library wanted to know. It was mainly mutiple choice questions with space for elaboration on each question. Demographic questions simply asked for department and job title. The surveys were distributed as interoffice memos so that each employee would get one. The vice president for research also asked the other departmental vice presidents to encourage their employees to answer it. Questionnaires were available in the library as well for those who needed a little encouragement and had not answered the original one.

The survey showed that employees wanted to learn more about the library but felt they did not have time. The only instruction they ever received was in informal, one-on-one conversations with the librarians. The work on search strategy for computer searches was seen as very useful beyond the individual search, and the SDI articles they received were useful for letting them know where information was available. Finding information on the computer was a top priority to people, followed by finding up-to-date industry and company information. Respondents did not give any useful answers to questions on the forum for instruction. Most of those who answered the survey were middle management from accounts or the creative departments.

Identifying Potential Programs

The librarians assessed their current instruction. The library had a few directional signs that worked well, but there were not enough of them. Individual help was given both in the library and in users' offices. The librarians wanted to reach more people through instruction, so although one-on-one help was viewed as helpful, the librarians decided to work on ways to reach groups.

The library staff got together to brainstorm and came up with programs and services they would like to incorporate into the project after evaluating the information from the needs assessment. They then asked the vice president for research to join their brainstorming session, both for good public relations and to bring in a corporate point of view.

The librarians searched the literature for help in planning their instruction program. They came up empty handed on advertising agencies and did not find much on special libraries, so they looked further for some more general plans and ideas they thought they could adapt. They also contacted some professional colleagues to see what others were doing with their libraries. Not much was being done, so they felt somewhat like pioneers and decided to take what help they could get and forge ahead.

Goals and Objectives

The librarians developed three goals after looking at all the information they had gathered. Under each are the corresponding objectives and strategies:

Goal 1. To bring the possibilities of information available through online sources to all employees.

1. All employees will be informed of new databases as they are available.

   A. Develop and distribute written information when new databases are released.

   B. For the most applicable databases, develop and schedule short group workshops about the databases as they become available.

2. All employees will become aware of the online searching the library provides and its results.

   A. Put out written information on the library's search service.

   B. Offer small group workshops explaining the online service, search strategy, and the kinds of information available. Hands-on practice time will be included to allow a better understanding of what the librarians do to get the online information and to create some excitement about the process.

Goal 2. To increase the knowledge of what information is available in the library itself.

1. The librarians will make their collection more accessible.

   A. Improve signage by implementing more signs in general and adding explanatory signs for specific areas.

B. Compile bibliographies of appropriate journal and reference book holdings and online services with industry information for each account.

2. Employees will learn what information is available in the library's reference collection.

   A. Formulate point-of-use instruction for the most used reference works.

   B. Develop written information and guides on the library's collection.

Goal 3. To increase the number of library users.

1. The librarians will use public relations techniques to advertise the library.

   A. Produce a newsletter to inform employees about the library, its sources, its services, and its staff.

   B. Consult with the public relations department about PR techniques.

   C. Produce the materials suggested by the public relations department.

2. The library will become part of the orientation of new employees.

   A. Work with the personnel director to become part of new employees' orientation to the company.

   B. Initiate a library tour for new employees.

   C. Create a small packet of informational materials for all new employees.

Working with the Administration

The librarians went with their proposal to the vice president for research. The needs assessment suggested that some instruction would be useful, but he was not convinced it was a necessary new endeavor for the library. The library, he felt, did a good job with its current work. However, the well-thought out goals and objectives excited him as he realized the value of what was being suggested, and they impressed him with the thorough way they responded to the needs assessment. He then took the proposal to the president and the other vice presidents. They were not all as enthusiastic, and the vice president for research knew he needed to bring in more support for the project. He got verbal support from the vice president for creative department, and asked the librarians to get written support from other employees in the targeted audiences. At that point, the president was willing to try two or three aspects of the program. Financial and personnel support was budgeted. Later, with the success of the first programs, the entire plan was approved and budgeted.

Staff Resources

From the beginning, the whole library staff was involved with the planning and implementation of this project. Everyone's tasks were in writing as part of the project. No new staff could be added, so the current staff took on the program in addition to their duties. Since time had to be made, each staff member clarified in writing what work was not getting done, and priorities of other library tasks were reassessed. Other employees also became involved in the project. An art director helped with graphics, the public relations department prepared publicity, and a copywriter helped prepare some of the written materials. Actual production of signs and written materials was also done outside the library.

Material Resources

The library decided to hold workshops in the company's conference room, so plans had to be made for scheduling. A computer with a modem had to be brought from the library, and a second one with a modem was found in the company so two stations would be available for hands-on practice. This was possible because the conference room has two phone lines. A workbook was identified to aid in teaching online searching, and several copies were bought on approval to see if the response to them warranted buying enough to give each employee attending the workshop. Novice searchers found them useful, so the workbook costs were permanently budgeted into the program.

Scheduling

The workshops evolved into two parts. A forty-five-minute presentation was scheduled for 10 a.m. to avoid conflicts for people who have to take care of early morning business, but not so late it interfered with lunch. The decision was to keep it short so participants would not feel they had lost the whole morning. The actual presentation took only a half hour, and the other fifteen minutes was allotted for mingling and questions. The workbooks were passed out then to be used as part of the presentation and to give participants a chance to use them in preparation for the afternoon session. The afternoon session started at 3 p.m. and lasted another forty-five minutes, with the first fifteen minutes spent on questions about the presentation, search strategy on particular topics, or the workbook. Then the participants were given hands-on practice with the help of the two librarians.

Tours were planned for 10 a.m. or 2 p.m. and lasted forty-five minutes. After the initial set of tours to current employees, they were given on an as-needed basis to new employees.

A monthly library newsletter was distributed in the middle of the month. Although no proof was available, the middle of the month seemed to be a short lull in the normal frantic activity, and the librarians hoped employees would pay more attention to the information then.

Mode of Instruction

Several modes of instruction were used as part of the program.

Tours: The library offered a series of tours intended to be an introduction to the library for all interested employees. Thereafter, the librarians worked with the personnel department to integrate the tours into the regular orientation of new employees.

Signage: Signs were added for several purposes. Some are directional and some label particular areas or sources. Care was taken to avoid having so many signs that they become confusing. Point-of-use instruction has also been implemented to explain how to use the card catalog, the serials file, the picture file, and certain reference works. These are concisely worded explanations on signs large enough to catch the user's attention, but not so big as to be overpowering.

Handouts: Bibliographies were being compiled on the book, journal, and online sources for each account. These are now distributed to everyone in the company who is in any way working on a particular product. As new employees are hired, they are immediately given the appropriate bibliographies. The bibliographies are designed to be easily updated so they are always timely. They are also displayed prominently in the library for users to take with them. In the beginning they were only available for the five biggest accounts. Additional bibliographies for other accounts and a general bibliography have been completed as time allows.

A commercially produced workbook was used in conjunction with the online workshop. Although it has proved to be a large financial investment, producing one would probably be equally expensive and use too much staff time.

Workshop: The online workshop was planned to allow interaction with more employees at one time. The workshop now consists of several modes of ground instruction—lecture, workbook, hands-on practice, and friendly mingling—to avoid boredom and too much of a classroom atmosphere.

Newsletter: This has proved to be an integral part of the library instruction program. It is one sheet, both sides, and issued monthly. Since it is simply typed on the word processor and duplicated in-house, it costs very little. Each employee receives it, and everyone on the library staff is encouraged to be involved in producing it.

Program Delivery

The underlying maxim of the instruction program continues to be brevity. Corporate employees are too busy to listen to or read anything that is too long. The librarians are willing to sacrifice content rather than lose employee participation.

Program Contents

The tours give the basic layout of the library, what is available, and what the library can do for users. The library staff also stresses that they are there to help the users with their information needs and they should feel free to call on the library any time. The whole staff is involved in the tours, with each staff member describing his or her duties as they affect the user. In the process of the tour, the librarians are able to explain about search strategy and how to use key reference works.

The directional signs are short, one or two words, and are planned only to give enough information for users to find what they need easily. The point-of-use signs try to explain briefly how to use particular sources. The sign on the card catalog clarifies what headings mean, how to use a divided catalog, what the various location symbols mean, and where resources are located that are not in the library. The serials file sign highlights the organization of the file, primarily holdings information. The sign for the picture file describes its organization and how to use the headings list to access its holdings. It also briefly states what can and cannot be found in the file. Signs are also made for heavily used reference works such as the advertising directories and Dun & Bradstreet. The signs explain the organization and use of the reference works as simply as possible.

As previously mentioned, the bibliographies include book, journal, and online sources. This includes both product and industry information for each account's product. Some of the information is repetitious, since accounts for milk, jam, and a snack food all need the same basic food sources. The bibliographic information is kept to a single side, with library hours, services, and policies on the back.

The workshops focus directly on online searching. The core of the workshop is search strategy and the role of the librarian in searching. Online sources can be of tremendous benefit to employees, but the librarians feel users have not taken full advantage of these databases because they have not known what to ask for or how to ask. Since the librarians do all the searching, the point of the workshop is not to train searchers, but to generate understanding about the capabilities of online information sources. The hands-on practice is included partly just to let users have some fun on the computer, but it also gives users some insight into what online searching entails. The librarians also foresee end-user searching and CD-ROM products in the library and hope these workshops help prepare them and their users. The ongoing workshops are planned to keep users up-to-date on new databases.

The newsletter is a very fluid tool, covering whatever the staff feels needs to be included. Primarily it is a vehicle for informing employees of new sources in all formats: new books and journals as well as new database availability. In addition, library news and policies are described. Information on library staff can show the human side of the library and try to break down stereotypes. Finally, the newsletter includes brief news reports that the librarians find while going through periodicals for SDI purposes that they think will be of interest and might otherwise be missed.

Evaluation

The workshops conclude with a written evaluation. It is very brief and, using multiple choice questions, asks attendees about the quality and usefulness of the various parts of the program. Open-ended questions solicit suggestions for improvements and for topics for future workshops. Early evaluations showed the arrangement of the afternoon workshop session was disappointing. Too many people wanted to use too few machines. The decision was made to divide the session into two groups, one at 1 p.m. and one at 3 p.m. Despite the time an extra workshop takes from regular library duties, the original arrangement did not work and so the instruction was not successful. Search strategy interests attendees as a topic, and the hands-on practice is a real hit. The workbook is useful in that it gives structure to the workshop, but attendees do not tend to work through the whole book. However, it is seen as a helpful reference tool for attendees to use to review something brought up in the workshop. The librarians interpret both the increased and the improved use of the service as an indication of the utility of the workshops.

Occasionally account executives bring a library bibliography with them to ask about a source, showing they actually read it and are finding it useful. The same is true of the newsletter, with users looking for the highlighted material or requesting the whole article from which the news item was pulled. Even the response from those who do not normally use the library is positive, indicating that they appreciate just knowing what is going on in a company department.

The response to the tours is more ambiguous. Some new employees are eager to get into the library and appreciate the orientation. Others feel it is a waste of time, although even some of them are pleasantly surprised at what the library can do for them and how much they learned.

The impact of the new signs is the most unclear. The directional signs may help, but behavior does not indicate such. The descriptive signs are probably not read, since the same questions are still being asked. After re-evaluating their use, the librarians have decided to leave them up for those who might use them, but wonder if users in the end still need the human touch and want to ask the librarian.

Although an instruction program in a library that does the research for its users may not seem important, the TLC program proved to be a success. Higher use of the library has resulted, as well as better use with more organized questions. Users benefit by getting more pertinent information because of the way they ask for it and it is easier for them to get because they have a better understanding of the structure of the library's research tools. Even clients have reported that account executives seem better prepared than before. The library boosted its public relations with the program and received recognition from upper management for the work they have done.

Botanical Garden

Type of Library

The library was established at the same time as the botanical garden. The highly specialized holdings are mainly horticultural and botanical, with smaller sections on related sciences, natural history, and local history. Besides a sizable collection of books and journals, the collection includes historical seed catalogs, reference sources on cards and microfiche, and a pamphlet and picture file. The library does not have access to any automated databases.

The library has two kinds of users: inside users from the scientific staff and the nursery, and outside users who are either amateurs—students and homeowners—or professional users such as landscape architects, freelance writers, artists, nursery owners, and gardeners. The library staff includes one full-time librarian, one part-time clerk, and three part-time volunteers. For outside users, the closed stacks are only accessible through the librarian.

Benefits of a Library Instruction Program

An instruction program would primarily make people more aware of the library, since many do not even know that it exists. More use would come from increased awareness. In-house staff and professional outside users might also save plants as well as time by identifying species, diseases, and pests more quickly and determining the appropriate care. Students should benefit from increased exposure to the variety of information sources available and that knowledge would be transferable to other libraries.

Needs Assessment

The librarian expanded her reference statistics to keep a fuller record of library use, including the general subject of information requested, how easily the information was found, sources used, the category of the user, and, when possible, the reason the information was needed. The librarian found that the questions were equally split between botanical and horticultural information. The botanical (identification) questions took the longest to answer, partly because the sources are more complicated and diverse. Professional users, especially in-house users, asked well-defined questions that made getting the resources easy. Students and homeowners needed more guidance in searching through the information.

The librarian very briefly surveyed all clients about how they used the library and what would make the information they wanted easier to find. Most users were happy with the library, but among the few suggestions were some good ideas for potential instruction. She also spoke at length to her department head, who proved to be not very helpful. But by letting him in on the process early in the planning stage and by asking for input, the librarian had an ally even if he did not actively support her initial plans.

Next, the librarian designed a written survey listing the possible instruction opportunities, asking people which would interest them and in what format. It was distributed to all garden employees and volunteers, to teachers who brought their classes to the botanical garden, and to other library users. The survey showed that newer employees were more interested in learning more about library sources and that long-term employees felt they were familiar enough with the library for their own needs. The two groups with the most positive response were the volunteers and the teachers. Other outside users wanted their questions answered, and because the stacks are closed, they felt the librarian is all the help they need to find the information.

Identifying Potential Programs

When current instruction activities were assessed, the library signs were found to range from very good to useless. A tour of the library was given to all new volunteers, but only to show them the places where volunteers work; it incorporated no information on how to use the library. The library had had a column in the botanical garden publication, but it had been usurped by the director who wanted to use the space for other articles. A brochure was subsequently developed, describing the library, its history, and some of its resources.

The librarian undertook a literature search on instruction and looked at articles on museum, corporate, and school libraries to cover the kinds of users of her library. General articles sometimes gave her an idea of what she could adapt for her own needs. She used her contacts in other botanical libraries as well as her local Special Libraries Association chapter to get suggestions and pointers.

Finally, the librarian classified the users of the botanical garden and determined who would be good potential audiences for instruction. She pinpointed volunteers, especially new ones; new employees; teachers with their classes; participants in children's program; adult education attendees; and sporadic outside users. She also assessed the library functions that could be enhanced by library instruction. Although finding information for users is the main public service function, outreach was seen as the most useful purpose for the instruction project.

Goals and Objectives

Two goals emerge as the basis for the instruction, each with supporting objectives:

Goal 1. To let potential users know of the library's existence, encourage them to seek information on plants, and help them learn how to use the resources.

1. Employees and volunteers will have library orientation.

   A. Current employees and volunteers will have an opportunity to come to a program about the library.

   B. An introduction to the library will be part of new employees orientation.

   C. Each new group of volunteers will receive instruction in the library.

2. Students will learn about the library and its resources.

   A. Teachers will bring classes to the library during field trips to the botanical garden.

   B. The librarian will explain how to find basic plant information and show some of the more interesting resources.

3. Children will be introduced to plant information.

   A. The librarian will go to the children's classes held at the garden.

   B. She will talk about finding plant information and highlight some of the children's books in the library collection.

4. The library will use written material to publicize the library and inform users.

   A. The library will create bookmarks illustrating sources on particular plants or topics.

   B. The library will have a column in the botanical garden magazine.

   C. The library will provide bibliographies to the adult education participants.

5. The library will improve its signs.

   A. Larger identification signs will be used.

   B. Better point-of-use instruction will be designed for the card catalog.

   C. Point-of-use instruction will be designed for major reference works.

Goal 2. To increase the library's involvement with other departments.

1. The library will work with the education department.

    A. The library will have a small part in the children's program.

    B. The library will be involved in the tours given to visiting school classes.

    C. The library will coordinate bibliographies for the adult education program.

2. The library will work with the volunteer office.

    A. Volunteers will receive an orientation to the library so they can use the library as needed in their volunteer activities.

    B. Volunteers will be encouraged to use the library.

Working with the Administration

The librarian went to her department head armed with her needs assessment information, her identification of potential programs, her goals and objectives, and her reputation; she hoped for the best. He was very cool to the idea in general and absolutely negative about some of the particular plans. The director did not like signs at all, so that suggestion was completely rejected. He also would not allow a library column in the garden magazine. However, the librarian felt a precedent had been set in the past with a library column, and the opportunity might present itself again in the future if any changes occurred in the administration or the magazine. After conferring with the other departments involved, the director would consider the orientations and presentations. The bookmarks and bibliographies were approved.

The librarian then went to the education department. The proposal was again coolly received. The children's program was completely rejected; the children are in a distant part of the garden for their program, and they actually work on a model garden. A presentation by the librarian was felt to be both inappropriate and too difficult to coordinate. The education specialist felt the children on the school tours would not be interested in going indoors to listen to a library program, but she begrudgingly gave the library ten minutes of time on the tour on a trial basis. Continuation would depend on evaluation of the program. The education specialist was interested in, if not enthusiastic about, the bibliographies.

The volunteer office was much more positive. They felt that the more that could be offered to the volunteers, the more they would get in return for their volunteer work at the garden. An orientation by the library for new volunteers as well as a program for current volunteers was endorsed.

The personnel department made no decision on the proposal, but rather sent it to the various departments for approval. The scientific and nursery departments were interested in a library orientation for their department employees. Continuation of the program, however, would depend on the evaluations and interest of employees.

Staff Resources

Because the library is a one-person library, the librarian has to rely on help from outside. She was able to get another volunteer to help her work on part of the project. She also got support from the publications department in producing the bookmarks and bibliographies. They created the graphics for the bookmarks, which have been carried over as a logo for the bibliographies.

Material Resources

The librarian is given a lump sum in her budget by the director and assistant director, and she has complete control over expenditures. This gave her certain fiscal freedom in planning her project. The only cost is the production of the bookmarks, signs, and bibliographies, but the publications department provides the material needed, supplying the heavy stock paper for the bookmarks and whatever printing needs to be done.

Scheduling

The only scheduling over which the librarian has any control is for the school tours. She asked to be towards the end of the tour. The children were too restless to listen indoors about books at the beginning of the field trip. The library is at the entrance/exit, so it is a logical stop on the way out, and the children may be interested in learning where to find more information after they have been on the tour. She also asked the education department to distribute the bibliographies at the beginning of the adult education program to make sure people would get them as part of whatever other literature they receive.

No scheduling needs to be done with new employees or volunteers. Whenever they are brought by the library for an orientation is acceptable, with some advance notice. She did plan one program for current employees and volunteers. It was planned for the morning when most people would be around, but nothing else has been scheduled.

Mode of Instruction

A tour or orientation is presented rather than an in-depth program because one goal of the instruction project is to provide awareness of the existence of the library, not actually to teach users how to use individual resources. The other goal is cooperation with other departments, and the librarian does not want to impinge on anyone's area. Finally, the children do not have the attention span for a long program and may not come back to the library, but the librarian wants them to know that information is available and to stimulate them to go after it.

The bibliographies are also planned to encourage the participants to go beyond the botanical garden program to find further information on their own. Those coming to an adult education program are not interested in listening to a lecture about the library, but the librarian hopes they will appreciate a guide to which they can refer when they need more information. If they choose to search for information in the library, the bibliographies have achieved the first goal, and at that point the librarian can do more one-on-one instruction. If they go to another library, the bibliography has still achieved the purpose of promoting an interest in further learning.

The bookmarks, like the bibliographies, are planned to be something that can be taken and consulted after leaving the botanical garden. The format was chosen partly as a gimmick that would encourage people to pick one up, and partly because as a bookmark it would continue to remind people that more information is available.

Program Delivery

Brevity is most important to all the components of the instruction project. The students are not eager to spend much time listening to the librarian after being outdoors touring the garden. Volunteers and employees have their responsibilities and can spare little time from when they need to get on with their work. Better signage and point-of-use instruction should help them be more independent and efficient. The bibliographies need to be short to avoid overwhelming the participants, and the bookmarks, of course, are limited by the design itself.

Program Contents

The children's tour covers information identifying plants and caring for them. The librarian brings out some of the most interesting illustrated books and some books written for children from the collection. She relates some of the information available to questions the children raise after their outdoor tour. She explains how to find some answers and lays the books out on the tables so the children can look at them.

The program for volunteers and employees emphasizes library research tools and library services. Some basic sources, as well as some of the more unique and interesting ones, are described and displayed. In the process the method of looking for plant information is integrated into the program.

The bibliographies include books and journals related to the topics of the seminars. Titles are annotated to give those attending the seminars a way to judge which of the sources will be useful and to pique their interest in pursuing more

information. They are no longer than one side of a page with the back used for information about the library. Because some sources are basic and some of the classes overlap topics, the librarian is able to use some of the annotations for more than one bibliography. The bookmarks are by design very brief, describing one or two sources on the topics of greatest interest to the outside patrons, such as roses, camellias, or cacti. They include information on library hours as well.

Publicity

Notices for orientations are sent to each employee and volunteer individually. They are also posted in the library. The bibliographies are announced and distributed towards the beginning of the class. The bookmarks are displayed prominently throughout the library.

Evaluation

Short, written evaluations, designed for each group of library orientation participants—the employees/volunteers and the school teachers—ask questions about relevancy, usefulness, presentation, and scheduling, and leave room for comments. The employees/volunteers evaluation also asks if the orientation will help them in their jobs. The teachers are asked if they will be encouraging their students to use the library and for what.

Volunteers have shown more interest than employees, both in attendance and on the evaluation. After the first program for employees, the instruction became basically one-on-one tutorials as new employees are hired, so the presentation has been changed to reflect an individual focus rather than a classroom atmosphere. The presentation for the volunteers has stayed basically the same, since they continue to come in groups. The scheduling remains flexible on an as-needed basis.

The only evaluation of the bibliographies and bookmarks is subjective observation: listed sources are requested more, showing that people are actually looking at the listings. Bookmarks on other topics will be printed and revisions made as time allows, but for the time being the bookmarks will remain as they are. The bibliographies have become more work than expected, so the seminars for which the librarian develops bibliographies will be chosen more judiciously and bibliographies reused whenever possible.

In looking at the program as a whole, the librarian feels she has accomplished her main goal of making people more aware of the library. Volunteers in particular are using it more in their tasks at the botanical garden. Other departments, particularly the publications and education departments, have become more involved in the library. Finally, the librarian hopes she has touched some students and interested them in finding more information on plants.

BIBLIOGRAPHY

Axelroth, J. L. "Library Instruction in the Private Law Firm Environment." *Legal Reference Services Quarterly* 5, No. 2/3 (1985): 117-76.

Brooke, A. "Some User Education Techniques Appropriate to Special Libraries." *Australian Special Libraries News* 13, No. 1 (1980): 15-18.

Ginn, D., P. E. Pinkowski, and W. T. Tylman. "Evaluation of an End-user Training Program." *Bulletin of the Medical Library Association* 75, No. 2 (1987): 117-21.

Graves, K. J., and S. A. Selig. "Library Instruction for Medical Students." *Bulletin of the Medical Library Association* 74, No. 2 (1986): 126-30.

Hubbard, A., and B. Wilson. "An Integrated Information Management Education Program: Defining a New Role for Librarians in Helping End-users." *Online* 10, No. 2 (1986): 15-23.

Kirk, C. L. "End-user Training at the Amoco Research Center." *Special Libraries* 77, No. 1 (1986): 20-27.

Lescohier, R. S., M. A. Lavin, and M. K. Landsberg. "Database Development and End-user Searching: Exxon Research and Engineering Company." In *Serving End-Users in Sci-tech Libraries*, E. Mount, ed. New York: Haworth Press, 1984.

Schildhauer, C. "Bibliographic Instruction I: Development of an Instructional Program." Paper presented at the Annual Meeting of the Special Libraries Association, Chemistry Libraries Division, Kansas City, Missouri, June, 1978. [ERIC Document Reproduction Service no. ED 174 250].

Schwartz, D. G. "Bibliographic Instruction: A Public Relations Perspective." *Medical Reference Services Quarterly* 3, No. 2 (1984): 43-49.

Staff, S. S., and B. L. Renford. "Evaluation of a Program to Teach Health Professionals to Search MEDLINE." *Bulletin of the Medical Library Association* 75, No. 3 (1987): 193-201.

Texas Library Association. Proceedings of the Seminar on User Education Activities, The State of the Art in Texas, Houston, Texas, April, 1976. [ERIC Document Reproduction Service no. ED 138 247].

Wygant, A. C. "Teaching End User Searching in a Health Sciences Center." In *End User Searching in the Health Sciences*, M. S. Wood, E. B. Horak, and B. Snow, eds. New York: Haworth Press, 1986.

PART VI
BIBLIOGRAPHY

ALA Goals Award
Bibliography

PREFACE

The subject of library or bibliographic instruction has proliferated greatly in the last decade. It has come to mean any kind of learning activity that occurs in a library or that focuses on skills for using a library or any of the specific resources and materials found in a library. The instruction is usually done by a librarian and may occur in many kinds of environments, including classrooms, via cable television, or individual sessions with a library user. Equally diverse are the ways in which the instruction is conducted: audiovisual resources, handouts, specific courses, signage, and many other variations.

This bibliography is not exhaustive, but it surveys a variety of current material and some earlier important citations, which have appeared in the journal literature, books, conference proceedings, media, and dissertations. This classified listing identifies sources, most published recently, on how academic, public, school, and special libraries and librarians have treated the subject of library and bibliographic instruction.

Additional, shorter lists of references by specific type of library follow each section in the handbook.

We hope that readers will discover new and useful sources in these and note some of the inventory material written for types of libraries other than their own.

JULIA GELFAND
University of California
Irvine, California

THELMA H. TATE
Douglass College
Rutgers University
New Brunswick, New Jersey

GENERAL OVERVIEW

Adams, Mignon S., and Jacquelyn M. Morris. *Teaching Library Skills for Academic Credit*. Phoenix, Ariz.: Oryx Press, 1985.

Alire, Camila A. "A Nationwide Survey of Education Doctoral Students' Attitudes Regarding the Importance of the Library and the Need for Bibliographic Instruction." Ph.D. diss., University of Northern Colorado, 1984.

Bolt, Janice H. "A Study of the Effects of a Bibliographic Instruction Course on Achievement and Retention of College Students." Ph.D. diss., Florida State University, 1986.

Carr, Jo Ann. *Minimum Library Use Skills: Standards, Test and Bibliography*. Madison, Wis.: Wisconsin Library Association, 1984.

Clark, Alice S. et al. *Teaching Librarians to Teach*. Metuchen, N.J.: Scarecrow Press, 1986.

Committee on Bibliography and Information Services for the Social Sciences and Humanities. *Information in Bibliography*. Ottawa: National Library of Canada, 1985.

Cowley, John, and Nancy Hammond. *Educating Information Users in Universities, Polytechnics and Colleges*. London: British Library Research and Development Department, 1987.

Dale, Sheila, and Joan Carty. *Finding Out about Continuing Education: Sources of Information and Their Use*. Philadelphia: Open University Press, 1985.

Fernandez, Georgina. "Pretest-Posttest Evaluation of Course Integrated Library Instruction in a Community College: A Critique of an Experiment." Ph.D. diss., University of New York at Albany, 1985.

Frick, Elizabeth, ed. *A Place to Stand: User Education in Canadian Libraries*. Ottawa: Canadian Library Association, 1988.

Goodin, M. Elspeth. "The Transferability of Library Research Skills from High School to College." Ph.D. diss., Rutgers University, 1987.

Kirk, Thomas G. *Teaching How to Teach Science Reference Materials: A Workshop for Librarians Who Serve the Undergraduate*. Chicago: Association of College and Research Libraries, American Library Association, 1984.

Kirkendall, Carolyn A., ed. *Marketing Instructional Services: Applying Private Sector Techniques to Plan and Promote Bibliographic Instruction*. Ann Arbor, Mich.: Pierian Press, 1986.

Lubans, John, ed. *Educating the Public Library User*. Chicago: American Library Association, 1983.

McNally, Thomas. *Creative Approaches to Video for Bibliographic Instruction*. Chicago: Association of College and Research Libraries, American Library Association, 1985.

Mellon, Constance A. *Bibliographic Instruction: The Second Generation*. Littleton, Colo.: Libraries Unlimited, Inc., 1987.

Michaels, Carolyn L., and Carolyn D. Clugston. *Library Literacy Means Lifelong Learning*. Metuchen, N.J.: Scarecrow Press, 1985.

Nielsen, Brian et al. *Educating the Online Catalog User: A Model for Instructional Development and Evaluation*. Evanston, Ill.: Northwestern, 1985.

Svinicki, Marilla D., and Barbara A. Schwartz. *Designing Instruction for Library Users: A Practical Guide*. New York: M. Dekker, 1988.

Toor, Ruth, and Hilda K. Weisburg. *Sharks, Ships & Potato Chips: Curriculum Integrated Library Instruction*. Berkeley Heights, N.J.: Library Learning Resources, Inc., 1986.

Valiukenas, Delija J. *Writing with Authority: A Guide to the Research Process*. New York: Random House, 1987.

Wolf, Carolyn E., and Richard Wolf. *Basic Library Skills*. 2nd ed. Jefferson, N.C.: McFarland & Co., 1986.

PLANNING INSTRUCTION PROGRAMS IN PUBLIC LIBRARIES

Automating Wisconsin Libraries. Report of the Council on Library and Network Development to the State Superintendent of Public Instruction. Madison, Wis.: Wisconsin State Department of Public Instruction, Division of Library Services, 1987. ERIC ED 292 479.

Bell, Irene Wood, and J. E. Wieckert. *Basic Media Skills through Games*. 2nd ed. Littleton, Colo.: Libraries Unlimited, Inc., 1985.

Boegen, Anne, ed. *Young Adult Services Manual*. Tallahassee, Fla.: Florida State Library, 1986.

Glover, Peggy D. *Library Services for the Woman in the Middle*. Hamden, Conn.: Shoe String Press, 1985.

Katz, Bill, and Ruth Fraley. *Library Instruction and Reference Services*. New York: Haworth Press, 1984.

Library Programs. LSCA Programs: An Action Report. Washington, D.C.: Office of Educational Research and Improvement, 1988. ERIC ED 292 478.

Lubans, John, ed. *Educating the Public Library User*. Chicago: American Library Association, 1983.

Mallet, Jerry J., and Marian R. Bartch. *Elementary School Library Resource Kit*. West Nyack, N.Y.: Center for Applied Research in Education, Inc., 1984.

Malley, Ian. *The Basics of Information Skills Teaching*. London: Clive Bingley, 1984.

Michaels, Carolyn L. *Library Literacy Means Lifelong Learning*. Metuchen, N.J.: Scarecrow Press, 1985.

Minor, Barbara B. *Trends in School Library Media Research as Reflected in the ERIC Database, June 1981-December 1985*. Washington, D.C.: Office of Educational Research and Improvement, 1985. ERIC ED 284 595.

Seager, Andrew J. et al. *Check This Out: Library Program Models*. Hampton, N.H.: RMC Research Corp., 1987. ERIC ED 288 529.

Using Your Library Effectively. Minnetonka, Minn.: Hennepin County Library, 1987. ERIC ED 291 398.

Weingand, Darlene E. *The Organic Public Library*. Littleton, Colo.: Libraries Unlimited, Inc., 1984.

LIBRARY INSTRUCTION IN PUBLIC LIBRARIES

Articles

Carbone, Jerry. "Library Use Instruction in the Small and Medium Public Library: A Review of the Literature." *Reference Librarian* 10 (Spring/Summer 1984): 149-57.

Dietrich, Jerrolyn M. "Library Use Instruction for Older Adults." *Canadian Library Journal* 41 (August 1984): 203-8.

Ferstl, Kenneth L. "Not Just Librarians, but Teachers Too." *Catholic Library World* 59, No. 1 (July/August 1987): 16-18.

Foster, Jocelyn. "Computer-Assisted Instruction: Putting It to the Test." *Canadian Library Journal* 44 (June 1987): 161-68.

Gann, Daniel H. "The Lifelong Learning Movement and the Role of Libraries in the Past Decade: A Bibliographic Guide." *Public Libraries* 24 (Spring 1985): 6-12.

Hendley, Margaret. "User Education: The Adult Patron in the Public Library." *RQ* 24 (Winter 1984): 191-92.

Jones, Patrick, and Candace E. Morse. "What to Do When the World Book Is Missing: A Program of Public Library Instruction for High School Students." *RQ* 26, No. 1 (Fall 1986): 31-34.

Kinney, Elaine M. "Thirty Minutes and Counting: A Bibliographic Instruction Program." *Illinois Libraries* 70, No. 1 (January 1988): 36-37.

Miller, Gloria. "Public School and Public Library Cooperation: A Joint Venture." *School Library Media Activities Monthly* 3, No. 5 (January 1987): 26-28.

Ming, Marilyn, and Gary MacDonald. "Rural Library Training: Bridging the Distance Effectively." *Canadian Library Journal* 44, No. 2 (April 1987): 73-78.

Ubabanek, Val. "Inform: Library Information at Your Fingertips." *Information Technology and Libraries* 1, No. 4 (December 1982): 336-41.

Weibel, Marguerite Crowley. "Use the Public Library with Adult Literacy Students." *Journal of Reading* 27, No. 1 (October 1983): 62-65.

Young, Christina Carr. "Anatomy of a Technology Transfer: The National Commission on Libraries and Information Science Literacy Project." *Library Trends* 35, No. 2 (Fall 1986): 263-75.

LIBRARY INSTRUCTION IN ACADEMIC LIBRARIES

Books

Adams, Mignon S., and Jacquelyn M. Morris. *Teaching Library Skills for Academic Credit*. Phoenix, Ariz.: Oryx Press, 1985.

Association of College and Research Libraries. Bibliographic Instruction Section. *Evaluating Bibliographic Instruction*. Chicago: American Library Association, 1983.

Beaubien, Anne K. et al. *Learning the Library: Concepts and Methods for Effective Bibliographic Instruction*. New York: R. R. Bowker Company, 1982.

Bibliographic Instruction in Vermont Libraries: A Directory of Programs and Methods. Johnson, Vt.: Johnson State College, 1987. ERIC ED 288 561.

Bolt, Janice Havlicek. "A Study of the Effects of a Bibliographic Instruction Course on Achievement and Retention of College Students." Ph.D. diss., Florida State University, 1986.

Frick, Elizabeth, ed. *A Place to Stand: User Education in Canadian Libraries*. Ottawa: Canadian Library Association, 1988.

Kirk, Thomas G. *Teaching How to Teach Science Reference Materials: A Workshop for Librarians Who Serve the Undergraduate*. 2nd ed. Chicago: Association of College and Research Libraries, American Library Association, 1984.

Kirkendall, Carolyn A., ed. *Marketing Instructional Services: Applying Private Sector Techniques to Plan and Promote Bibliographic Instruction*. Ann Arbor, Mich.: Pierian Press, 1986.

McClintock, Marsha H., ed. *Training Users of Online Public Access Catalogs. Report of a Conference Sponsored by Trinity University and the Council on Library Resources (San Antonio, Texas, January 12-14, 1983)*. Washington, D.C.: Council on Library Resources, July 1983. ERIC ED 235 832.

Mellon, Constance A. *Bibliographic Instruction: The Second Generation*. Littleton, Colo.: Libraries Unlimited, Inc., 1987.

National Library of Canada. Committee on Bibliography and Information Services for the Social Sciences and Humanities. *Instruction in Bibliography*. Ottawa: National Library of Canada, 1985.

Nielsen, Brian et al. *Educating the Online Catalog User: A Model for Instructional Development and Evaluation*. Evanston, Ill.: Northwestern, 1985.

Oberman, Cerise, and Katina Strauch. *Theories of Bibliographies Education: Designs for Teaching*. New York: R. R. Bowker Company, 1982.

Svinicki, Marilla D., and Barbara Schwartz. *Designing Instruction for Library Users: A Practical Guide*. New York: M. Dekker, 1988.

Articles

Anthes, Susan H., and Lawson Crowe. "Teaching Library Literacy." *College Teaching* 35, No. 3 (Summer 1987): 92-94.

Ball, Mary A., and Molly Mahony. "Foreign Students, Libraries, and Culture." *College & Research Libraries* 48, No. 2 (March 1987): 160-61.

Baxter, Pam M. "The Benefits of In-Class Bibliographic Instruction." *Teaching of Psychology* 13, No. 1 (February 1986): 40-41.

Bechtel, Joan. "Developing and Using the Online Catalog to Teach Critical Thinking." *Information Technology and Libraries* 7, No. 1 (March 1988): 30-40.

Binkley, R. David, and James R. Parrott. "A Reference-Librarian Model for Computer-Aided Library Instruction." *Information Services and Use* 7, No. 1 (1987): 31-38.

Bradigan, Pamela S. et al. "Graduate Student Bibliographic Instruction at a Large University: A Workshop Approach." *RQ* 26 (Spring 1987): 335-40.

Brigham Young University. "Course Integrated Bibliographic Instruction Workshop. (1986: Brigham University) September 18-19, 1986." Two Videocassettes (1986): 120 minutes.

Broidy, Ellen. "Reference Librarian as Teacher: Ego, Ideal and Reality in a Reference Department." *Reference Librarian* 14 (Spring/Summer 1986): 159-71.

Dowell, Connie V. "Weaving Library Skills into the Curriculum." *RQ* 26 (Winter 1986): 165-67.

Feinberg, Richard, and Christine King. "Short-Term Library Skill Competencies: Arguing for the Achievable." *College & Research Libraries* 49, No. 1 (January 1988): 24-28.

Fields, Carolyn B. "Using the Results of a Pre-Test to Determine Lecture Content: A Case Study." *Research Strategies* 5 (Winter 1987): 29-35.

Gratch, Bonnie G. "Rethinking Instructional Assumptions in an Age of Computerized Information Access." *Research Strategies* 6, No. 1 (Winter 1988): 4-7.

Graves, Gail T., and Barbara K. Adams. "Bibliographic Instruction Workbooks: Assessing Two Models Used in a Freshman English Program." *Research Strategies* 6, No. 1 (1988): 18-24.

Huston, Mary M., and Susan L. Perry. "Information Instruction: Considerations for Empowerment." *Research Strategies* 5 (Spring 1987): 70-77.

Jakobovits, Leon A., and D. Nahl-Jakobovits. "Learning the Library: Taxonomy of Skills and Errors." *College & Research Libraries* 48 (May 1987): 203-14.

Johnson, Judy. "Application of Learning Theory to Bibliographic Instruction: An Annotated Bibliography." *Research Strategies* 6, No. 3 (Summer 1986): 138-41.

Kautz, Barbara A. et al. "The Evolution of a New Library Instruction Concept: Interactive Video." *Research Strategies* 6, No. 3 (1988): 109-77.

Kenney, Donald J., and Linda J. Wilson. "Developing a Partnership in Library Instruction." *College & Research Libraries News* 47, No. 5 (May 1986): 321-22.

Kohl, David F. "Effectiveness of Course-Integrated Bibliographic Instruction in Improving Coursework." *RQ* 27, No. 2 (Winter 1986): 206-11.

Kosuda, Kathleen. "Bibliographic Instruction at a Small Goal-Oriented Campus." *Catholic Library World* 58, No. 2 (September/October 1986): 86-87, 90.

McCarthy, Constance. "The Faculty Problem." *Journal of Academic Librarianship* 11, No. 3 (July 1985): 142-45.

"Model Statement of Objectives for Academic Bibliographic Instruction: Draft Revision." *College & Research Libraries News* 48, No. 5 (May 1987): 256-61.

Mularski, Carol. "Academic Library Service to Deaf Students: Survey and Recommendations." *RQ* 26, No. 4 (Summer 1987): 477-86.

Pask, Judith M. "Computer-Assisted Instruction for Basic Library Skills." *Library Software Review* 7, No. 1 (January/February 1988): 6-11.

Penhale, Sara J. "Integrating End-User Searching into a Bibliographic Instruction Program." *RQ* 27, No. 2 (Winter 1986): 212-20.

Segal, Joan S. "Identifying Needs and Solutions." *College & Research Libraries News* 48, No. 11 (December 1987): 717-19.

Selin, Heliane. "Teaching Research Methods to Undergraduates." *College Teaching* 36, No. 2 (Spring 1988): 54-56.

Shapiro, Beth J. "Library Use, Library Instruction and User Success." *Research Strategies* 5 (Spring 1987): 60-69.

Sheridan, Jean. "Andragogy: A New Concept for Academic Librarians." *Research Strategies* 4, No. 4 (Fall 1986): 156-57.

Shill, Harold B. "Bibliographic Instruction: Planning for the Electronic Information Environment." *College & Research Libraries* 48, No. 5 (September 1987): 433-53.

INSTRUCTION IN THE USE OF LIBRARIES IN SCHOOLS

Books

Carr, Jo Ann. *Minimum Library Use Skills: Standards, Test and Bibliography.* Madison, Wis.: Wisconsin Library Association, 1984.

Goodin, M. Elspeth. "The Transferability of Library Research Skills from High School to College." Ph.D. diss., Rutgers University, 1987.

Joyce, Darlene J. "The Effects of Library Curricula on Student Attitudes toward the Elementary Library." Ph.D. diss., Western Washington University, 1988.

Library Information Skills for Quality Education. Austin, Tex.: Texas Education Agency, 1987. ERIC ED 281 558.

Toor, Ruth, and Hilda K. Weisburg. *Sharks, Ships & Potato Chips: Curriculum Integrated Library Instruction.* Berkeley Heights, N.J.: Library Learning Resources, 1986.

Articles

Bhalla, Pam. "Modeling a Library Media-Classroom Integrated Instructional Process." *School Library Media Activities Monthly* 4, No. 1 (September 1987): 26-27.

Brophy, Edward, and Dennis M. Lynch. "Awareness and Access to Knowledge: Bibliographic Instruction: Search Strategy." *Catholic Library World* 58, No. 1 (July/August 1986): 35-41.

Burgess, Barbara J. "Researching Skills: They Need Them When They Need Them." *Catholic Library World* 59, No. 3 (November/December 1987): 116-17.

Caputo, Anne S. "Use of DIALOG's Classroom Instruction Program and Dow Jones News/Retrieval Service in the Classroom to Teach Online Searching." *Education Libraries* 11, No. 1 (Winter 1986): 5-15.

Cleaver, Betty P. "Thinking about Information Skills for Lifelong Learning." *School Library Media Quarterly* 16, No. 1 (Fall 1987): 29-31.

Craver, Kathleen W. "Use of Academic Libraries by High School Students: Implications for Research." *RQ* 27, No. 1 (Fall 1987): 53-66.

Eisenberg, Michael. "Managing the Library Information Skills Program: Developing Support Systems for Planning and Implementation." *School Library Media Activities Monthly* 2, No. 7 (March 1986): 27-33.

Fiebert, Elyse E. "The Integration of Online Bibliographic Instruction into the High School Library Curriculum." *School Library Media Quarterly* 13, No. 2 (Spring 1985): 96-99.

Hammond, Jean K. "Primary Research: A Program of Basic Research Skills for Primary Students." *School Library Media Activities Monthly* 3, No. 10 (June 1987): 26-29.

Kemp, Barbara E. et al. "Building a Bridge: Articulation Programs for Bibliographic Instruction." *College & Research Libraries* 47, No. 5 (September 1986): 470-74.

Kulthau, Carol C. "An Emerging Theory of Library Instruction." *School Library Media Quarterly* 16, No. 1 (Fall 1987): 23-28.

Kulthau, Carol C. "A Process Approach to Library Skills Instruction." *School Library Media Quarterly* 13, No. 1 (Winter 1985): 35-40.

Mancall, Jacqueline C. "Teaching Online Searching: A Review of Recent Research and Some Recommendations for School Media Specialists." *School Library Media Quarterly* 13, No. 3-4 (Summer 1985): 215-20.

Maushay, Jane A. "Take a Multidisciplinary Approach to Library Skills." *School Library Media Monthly* 4, No. 5 (January 1988): 24-27.

Nelson, Sandra M. "Modifying and Planning Library Media Skills Lessons for Exceptional Students." *School Library Media Monthly* 4, No. 5 (January 1988): 28-32.

O'Hanlon, Nancyanne. "Library Skills, Critical Thinking, and the Teacher-Training Curriculum." *College & Research Libraries* 48, No. 1 (January 1987): 17-26.

Patterson, Charles D. "Librarians as Teachers: A Component of the Educational Process." *Journal of Education for Library and Information Science* 28, No. 1 (Summer 1987): 3-8.

Rankin, Virginia. "One Route to Critical Thinking." *School Library Journal* 34, No. 5 (January 1988): 28-31.

Schon, Isabel et al. "A Special Motivational Intervention Program and Junior High School Student's Library Use and Attitudes." *Journal of Experimental Education* 53, No. 2 (Winter 1985): 97-101.

Sliney, Marjory. "Information Skills Teaching: A User Education Program in a Post-Primary School." *School Librarian* 33, No. 2 (June 1985): 115-20.

LIBRARY INSTRUCTION IN SPECIAL LIBRARIES

Kirk, Cheryl L. "End-User Training at the AMOCO Research Center." *Special Libraries* 77, No. 1 (Winter 1986): 20-27.

Kirkendall, Carolyn A., ed. *Marketing Instructional Services: Applying Private Sector Techniques to Plan and Promote Bibliographic Instruction.* Ann Arbor, Mich.: Pierian Press, 1986.

Lutzker, Marilyn, and Eleanor Ferral. *Criminal Justice Research in Libraries: Strategies and Resources.* New York: Greenwood Press, 1986.

Rader, Hannelore B. "Library Orientation and Instruction— 1985." *Reference Services Review* 14, No. 2 (Summer 1986): 59-69.

Shill, Harold B. "Bibliographic Instruction: Planning for the Electronic Information Environment." *College & Research Libraries* 48, No. 5 (September 1987): 433-53.

Sparks, Marie C. "A Dental Library Instruction Program." *Medical Reference Services Quarterly* 4, No. 3 (Fall 1985): 27-36.

PROGRAM PLANNING FOR LIBRARY INSTRUCTION

Brown, Doris R. "Three Terminals, a Telefax, and One Dictionary: Electronic Library Service as a Solution for an External Learning Center." *College & Research Libraries News* 46, No. 10 (November 1985): 538-46.

Chor Shing Lam, John. "An Encounter of the Massive Kind and a Friendly Interface." *IATUL Quarterly* 1, No. 1 (March 1987): 51-62.

deSilva, Rufus. "Open Learning in Library Instruction: A Case Study." *Education Libraries Bulletin* 30, No. 2 (Summer 1987): 15-24.

Hanson, Janet R. "Teaching Information Sources in Business Studies: An Application of the Theories of J. Bruner and R. M. Gagne." *Journal of Librarianship* 17, No. 3 (July 1985): 185-99.

Malley, Ian. *A Survey of Information Skills Teaching in Colleges of Further and Higher Education.* London: British Library, Research and Development Department, 1988.

Segal, JoAnn S. "Identifying Needs and Solutions." *College & Research Libraries News* 48, No. 11 (December 1987): 717-19.

Shill, Harold B. "Bibliographic Instruction: Planning for the Electronic Information Environment." *College & Research Libraries* 48, No. 5 (September 1987): 433-53.

Stankus, Tony. "The New O'Callahan Science Library at the College of the Holy Cross." *Science and Technology Libraries* 7, No. 1 (Fall 1986): 45-55.

Sugranes, Maria R. et al. "Computer Assisted Instruction Remediation Program for Credit Course in Bibliographic Instruction." *Research Strategies* 4, No. 1 (Winter 1986): 18-26.

GOALS AND OBJECTIVES

Bleasdale, Charles. "The Management of Change—The Mechanism and the Model." *Learning Resources Journal* 1, No. 1 (June 1985): 10-18.

Clow, David, and Clive Cochran. "User Education and Staff Training in a Continuing Education Programme." *Education for Information* 4, No. 1 (March 1986): 17-25.

Feinberg, Richard, and Christine King. "Short-Term Library Skill Competencies: Arguing for the Achievable." *College & Research Libraries* 49, No. 1 (January 1988): 24-28.

Hamilton, D. "Library Users and Online Systems—Suggested Objectives for Library Instruction." *RQ* 25, No. 2 (Winter 1985): 195-97.

Kendrick, Aubrey W. "BI for Business Students: Team Teaching at the University of Alabama." *College & Research Libraries* 46, No. 9 (October 1985): 482-83.

Maniez, Jacques. "Outline of a Methodology for Training in Librarianship." *Education for Information* 3, No. 1 (March 1985): 51-54.

Margolis, Michael. "Library Instruction and Intellectual Stimulation." *Reference Services Review* 15, No. 1 (Spring 1987): 47-49.

McNeer, Elizabeth J. "Administrator's Perspective on Library Instruction." *Journal of Library Administration* 6, No. 1 (Spring 1985): 65-69.

Miller, Connie, and Patricia Tegler. "In Pursuit of Windmills: Librarians and the Determination to Instruct." *Reference Librarian* 18 (Summer 1987): 119-34.

"Model Statement of Objectives for Academic Bibliographic Instruction: Draft Revision." *College & Research Libraries News* 48, No. 5 (May 1987): 256-61.

Nielsen, Brian, and Betsy Baker. "Educating the Online Catalog User: A Model Evaluation Study." *Library Trends* 35, No. 4 (Spring 1987): 571-85.

Schub, Sue. "Teaching Bibliographic Instruction." *Library Journal* 113, No. 2 (February 1988): 39-40.

TEACHING METHODS

Association of College and Research Libraries, Bibliographic Instruction Section. *Organizing and Managing a Library Instruction Program: Checklists.* Rev. ed. Chicago: Association of College and Research Libraries, 1986.

Berquist, Goodwin et al. "Coping with the Critical Essay in a Large Lecture Course." *Communication Education* 35, No. 4 (October 1986): 396-99.

Bibliographic Instruction, Vermont Libraries: A Directory of Programs and Methods. Johnson, Vt.: Johnson State College, 1987. ERIC ED 288 561.

Collins, Gayle et al. "Teaching Library Skills." *Book Report* 5, No. 4 (January/February 1987): 16-30.

Dickson, Laura K. et al. *New Start: Bibliographic Instruction for Nontraditional Students.* Omaha, Nebr.: University Library, 1987. ERIC ED 288 527.

Ferstl, Kenneth L. "Not Just Librarians, but Teachers Too." *Catholic Library World* 59, No. 1 (July/August 1987): 16-18.

Kissinger, Pat. "Library Evaluation Services." *Education Libraries* 12, No. 2 (Spring 1987): 44-47.

Kohl, David F., and Lizabeth A. Wilson. "Effectiveness of Course Integrated Bibliographic Instruction in Improving Coursework." *RQ* 27, No. 2 (Winter 1986): 206-11.

Kosuda, Kathleen. "Bibliographic Instruction at a Small Goal-Oriented Campus." *Catholic Library World* 58, No. 2 (September/October 1986): 86-87.

Lynch, M. Dennis. "Awareness and Access to Knowledge: Bibliographic Instruction: Search Strategy." *Catholic Library World* 58, No. 1 (July/August 1986): 39-41.

MacAdam, Barbara. "Humor in the Classroom: Implications for the Bibliographic Instruction Librarian." *College & Research Libraries* 46, No. 4 (July 1985): 327-33.

Markman, Marsha C., and Gordon B. Leighton. "Exploring Freshman Composition Student Attitudes about Library Education Sessions and Workbooks: Two Studies." *Research Strategies* 5, No. 3 (Summer 1987): 126-34.

Mealy, Virginia et al. "Sharing Skills." *School Library Media Activities Monthly* 4, No. 1 (September 1987): 32-36.

Nahl-Jakobovits, Diane, and Leon A. Jakobovits. "Managing the Affective Micro-Information Environment." *Research Strategies* 3, No. 1 (Winter 1985): 17-28.

Riedl, Richard. "Computer Communications Problems: How to Teach Your Students to Overcome Them." *School Library Media Activities Monthly* 3, No. 4 (December 1986): 29-32, 50.

Sampson, Anne. *Good Book Lookers: A Three-Week Introductory Module in the Language Arts to Foster Independent Reading among Third Graders.* Teaching Guide No. 052, 1988. ERIC ED 292 056.

SantaVicca, Edmund F. "Teaching Research Skills in Linguistics: An Interdisciplinary Model for the Humanities and the Social Sciences." *Research Strategies* 4, No. 4 (Fall 1986): 168-76.

Sheridan, Jean. "Andragogy: A New Concept for Academic Librarians." *Research Strategies* 4, No. 4 (Fall 1986): 156-57.

EVALUATION OF LIBRARY INSTRUCTION

Adams, Mignon, Mary H. Loe, and Mark Morey. *Evaluating a Library Instruction Program: A Case Study of Intra-campus Cooperation.* Oswego, N.Y.: SUNY College at Oswego, 1983. ERIC ED 274 378.

Berkowitz, Robert E. et al. "When Information Skills Meet Science Curriculum: A Cooperative Effort." *School Library Media Activities Monthly* 4, No. 10 (June 1988): 28-33.

Bhalla, Pam. "Modeling a Library Media-Classroom Integrated Instruction Process." *School Library Media Activities Monthly* 4, No. 1 (September 1987): 26-27.

Bradigan, Pamela S. et al. "Graduate Student Bibliographic Instruction at a Large University: A Workshop Approach." *RQ* 26, No. 3 (Spring 1987): 335-40.

Cheney, Paul H., and R. Ryan Nelson. "A Tool for Measuring and Analyzing End User Computing Abilities." *Information Processing and Management* 24, No. 2 (1988): 199-203.

Franklin, Karen, comp. *Instruction in Bibliography. Report of the Survey of Bibliographic Instruction in Selected Departments of Canadian Universities, 1982/83.* Ottawa: National Library of Canada. ERIC ED 266 801.

Frick, Elizabeth. "Professional Training for User Education: The U.K." *Journal of Education for Library and Information Science* 28, No. 1 (Summer 1987): 26-37.

Gratch, Bonnie. "Toward a Methodology for Evaluating Research Paper Bibliographies." *Research Strategies* 3, No. 4 (Fall 1985): 170-77.

Graves, Gail T., and Barbara K. Adams. "Bibliographic Instruction Workbooks: Assessing Two Models Used in a Freshman English Program." *Research Strategies* 6, No. 1 (Winter 1988): 18-24.

Greenfield, Louise, et al. *University of Arizona Library. A Final Report from the Public Services Research Projects. Assessing the Instructional Needs of Students in a Selected Scientific Discipline at the University of Arizona.* Tucson, Ariz.: Arizona University Library; Washington, D.C.: Association of Research Libraries; Office of Management Studies, January 1985.

Hanson, Elizabeth, and Judith Serebnick. "Evaluation of the Public Service Function of Serial File Systems." *College & Research Libraries* 47, No. 6 (November 1986): 575-76.

Hardesty, Larry. *Evaluation of Bibliographic Instruction.* Paper presented at the Library Instruction Round Table of the Alabama Library Association, Montgomery, Ala., 9 April 1986. ERIC ED 271 115.

Haws, Rae. "An Attitudinal Study of Students toward a Required Library Course." *Research Strategies* 5, No. 4 (Fall 1987): 172-79.

Jacobson, Frances F. "Issues in the Implementation of an Information-Gathering Competency Requirement in Business." *Research Strategies* 5, No. 1 (Winter 1987): 18-28.

Kaplowitz, Joan. "A Pre- and Post-Test Evaluation of the English 3-Library Instruction Program at UCLA." *Research Strategies* 4, No. 1 (Winter 1986): 11-17.

Kissinger, Pat. "Library Evaluation Services." *Education Libraries* 12, No. 2 (Spring 1987): 44-47, 53.

Larson, Mary Ellen, and Dace Freivalds. *Pennsylvania State University Libraries: A Final Report from the Public Services Research Projects: The Effect of an Instruction Program on Online Catalog Users.* Washington, D.C.: Association of Research Librarians, Office of Management Studies, Pennsylvania State University Libraries, 1985. ERIC ED 255 223.

Larson, Mary Ellen, and Ellen Meltzer. "Education for Bibliographic Instruction." *Journal of Education for Library and Information Science* 28, No. 1 (Summer 1987): 9-16.

Markuson, Carolyn. "Making It Happen: Taking Charge of the Information Curriculum." *School Library Media Quarterly* 15, No. 1 (Fall 1986): 37-40.

McDonough, Kristin. "Identifying Key Works in a Field: The Package Approach." *Research Strategies* 5, No. 1 (Winter 1987): 4-17.

Mellon, Constance A. "Attitudes: The Forgotten Dimension in Library Instruction." *Library Journal* 113, No. 4 (1988): 137-39.

Nielsen, Brian, and Betsy Baker. "Educating the Online Catalog User: A Model Evaluation Study." *Library Trends* 35, No. 4 (1987): 571-85.

Pask, Judith M. "Computer-Assisted Instruction for Basic Library Skills." *Library Software Review* 7, No. 1 (January/February 1988): 6-11.

Robbins-Carter, Jane, and Douglass L. Zweizig. "Are We There Yet? Evaluating Library Collections, Reference Services, Programs, and Personnel." *American Libraries* 17, No. 1 (January 1986): 32, 34, 36.

Ward, Sandra N. "Course-Integrated DIALOG Instruction." *Research Strategies* 3, No. 2 (Spring 1985): 52-64.

Ware, Susan A., and Deena J. Morganti. "A Competence-Based Approach to Assessing Workbook Effectiveness." *Research Strategies* 4, No. 1 (Winter 1986): 4-10.

Wheeler, Helen Rippier. *For Credit, Undergraduate, Bibliographic Instruction Courses in the University of California System: With Consideration of the Berkeley Campus' Bibliography 1 Course-Program's History as a Model.* Berkeley, Calif.: University of Berkeley Library, 1986. ERIC ED 266 799.

Wilson, Lizabeth A. "Education for Bibliographic Instruction: Combining Practice and Theory." *Journal of Education for Library and Information Science* 28, No. 1 (Summer 1987): 17-25.

COST OF BIBLIOGRAPHIC INSTRUCTION

Caputo, Ann S. et al. "Use of DIALOG's Classroom Instruction Program and Dow Jones News/Retrieval Service in the Classroom to Teach Online Searching: Annotated ERIC Bibliography." *Education Libraries* 11, No. 1 (Winter 1986): 5-10.

Everhart, Nancy. *MMI Preparatory School Computerized Model Library.* Freeland, Pa.: MMI Preparatory School, 1986. ERIC ED 291 389.

Fayen, Emily Gallup. *Microcomputers and the Online Catalog: Changing How the Catalog Is Used.* A paper presented at the annual meeting of the American Library Association, New York, 30 June 1986.

Sugranes, Maria R., and Larry C. Snider. "Microcomputer Applications for Library Instruction: Automation of Test and Assignment Scoring, and Student Record Keeping." *Microcomputers for Information Management* 2, No. 3 (September 1985): 171-88.

Tenopir, Carol. "Online Education: Planning for the Future." *Online* 11 (January 1987): 65-66.

Tenopir, Carol. "Online Searching in Schools." *Library Journal* 111, No. 2 (1986): 60-61.

MARKETING/PUBLICITY FOR LIBRARY INSTRUCTION

Berkowitz, Robert E. et al. "Public Relations: Building Support for the School Library." *Book Report* 6, No. 1 (May/June 1987): 12-23.

Caswell, Lucy S. "Building a Strategy for Academic Library Exhibits." *College & Research Libraries* 46, No. 4 (April 1985): 165-66, 168.

Christou, Corilee, and Donald Dyal. "Marketing the Information Center: A Blueprint for Action and Getting It Airborne." *Wilson Library Bulletin* 62, No. 8 (April 1988): 35-40.

Hill, John W. "Using Chemical Principles to Encourage Critical Thinking in Consumer Chemistry." *Journal of Chemical Education* 65, No. 3 (March 1988): 209-10.

Hubbard, Abigail, and Barbara Wilson. "An Integrated Information Management Education Program ... Defining a New Role for Librarians in Helping End-Users." *Online* 10, No. 2 (1986): 15-23.

Jacobson, Frances F. "Issues in the Implementation of an Information-Gathering Competency Requirement in Business." *Research Strategies* 5, No. 1 (Winter 1987): 18-28.

Jones, Ann D., and Eleanor Stevens. "Library Assignments in Undergraduate Business Courses: A Simplified Approach." *Bulletin of the Association for Business Communication* 49, No. 3 (September 1986): 13-16.

Markuson, Carolyn. "Making It Happen: Taking Charge of the Information Curriculum." *School Library Media Quarterly* 15, No. 1 (Fall 1986): 37-40.

Thesing, Jane I. "Marketing Academic Library Bibliographic Instruction Programs: Case and Commentary." *Research Strategies* 3, No. 1 (Winter 1985): 29-36.

Appendix A: World Book—
ALA Goals Award

In June 1985, the Library Instruction Round Table (LIRT) was awarded the World Book—American Library Association Goals Award for a proposal titled "Developing Programs in Library Use Instruction for Lifelong Learning." The proposal involved the creation of a handbook for librarians in all types of libraries who are interested in developing a library use instruction program at their institution. According to the proposal, "The use of a structured process for organizing an instruction program would involve staff and/or faculty, administrator, student, and other user support. At the same time, consistency in the organization of programs would provide a framework for the eventual development of an articulated curriculum at all levels and between all types of libraries. To develop such a program would require the cooperation among the various types of libraries and a consistent organization of the content of instruction programs—all organized with a similar goal—the continuous growth of the individual's information retrieval and handling skills concurrent with their chronological and intellectual growth" (Brottman "Goal Award").

Thus, the project was to have two purposes:

1. To develop techniques for organizing and implementing library use instruction programs that are applicable to their particular level, but are also consistent in their goals, objectives, and techniques.

2. To develop a model training program for persons and institutions interested in developing a library use instruction program. Such a program could further ensure quality and consistency.

The overall plan was to:

1. Survey librarians from different types of libraries regarding their needs and/or the problems they have encountered in developing library use instruction programs in their institutions.

2. Develop a handbook which delineates the steps and provides the necessary guidelines for involving staff, faculty, administrators, students and other library users in the design of an instruction program.

3. Offer a two-day preconference training institute for a minimum of thirty librarians from all types of libraries. The criteria for the selection of institute attendees will be developed as a result of the responses to the survey. These librarians will go through the steps described in the handbook and they will develop a library use instruction program for their library with the assistance of the group leaders.

4. The outcome of the institute would be to test and modify the handbook so that it can be used by others.

The first step was to recruit librarians, with a variety of talents and a willingness to be committed to the project and to work on each of the various aspects of the project. Of the forty-three persons asked to serve and be responsible for specific parts of the project, only three were unable to accept.

Once all of the persons agreed to serve, various responsibilities were designated. The first step was to conduct a random survey of librarians in each of the different types of libraries: school, academic, junior college, public, and special. The surveys were written by Lois Pausch from the University of Illinois at Urbana and Mary Pagliero-Popp from Indiana University at Bloomington. Over 2,600 surveys were mailed and the return in some cases was over 65 percent. At the same time Julia Gelfand from the University of California at Irvine and Thelma Tate at the Douglass Campus of Rutgers University in New Brunswick, New Jersey, began an extensive literature search in all of the databases and indexes that might have references to sources related to bibliographic instruction. After compiling the bibliography (which has since been updated to the end of 1988) they also accumulated articles that were sent to each of the groups writing a specific section of the handbook.

Once the surveys were returned, they were tallied and summarized by Barbara Ford-Foster at Bowling Green State University in Bowling Green, Ohio, and Robert Kuhner of the City College Library in New York City. The compilations of the surveys were distributed to each member of the committee.

The next step was the writing of the first draft of the handbook. The surveys and the literature searches were completed and sent to each of the respective groups responsible for the writing of each section. The completed first drafts were brought to the midwinter meeting where each group critiqued the writing of every other group. Suggestions were made for clarification and revision with the entire handbook to be complete before the annual American Library Association conference in June 1986. Feedback from the ALA preconference institute was incorporated in a second revision of the handbook, so this end product truly reflects the writing and experience of literally hundreds of library instructors.

LIRT GOALS AWARD COMMITTEE

DIRECTOR

May Brottman, Media Specialist
Glenbrook North High School
Northbrook, Illinois

CONSULTANT

Patricia Breivik, Director
Towson State University
Towson, Maryland

Critique and Advisory Group

ACADEMIC LIBRARY

Mignon Adams, Director
Joseph W. England Library
Philadelphia College of Pharmacy and Science
Philadelphia, Pennsylvania

COMMUNITY COLLEGE

Kathy Jordan, Instructional Services Librarian
Northern Virginia Community College
Alexandria, Virginia

SCHOOL LIBRARY

Fran Corcoran, IMC Coordinator
School District #62
Des Plaines, Illinois

PUBLIC LIBRARY

Helen T. Burns, Director
Elsie Quirk Public Library
Englewood, Florida

SPECIAL LIBRARY

Tobeylynn Birch, Director
California School of Professional Psychology
Los Angeles, California

SECRETARY AND ADMINISTRATIVE ASSISTANT

Georgeanne Moore
Glenbrook North High School
Northbrook, Illinois

SURVEY DESIGNERS

Lois Pausch
Math/Statistics Library
University of Illinois
Urbana, Illinois

Mary Pagliero-Popp
Undergraduate Library
Indiana University at Bloomington
Bloomington, Indiana

SURVEY COMPILATION

Robert Kuhner
Library
City College of New York (CUNY)
New York, New York

Barbara Ford-Foster, Reference Librarian
Bowling Green State University
Bowling Green, Ohio

LITERATURE SEARCH AND BIBLIOGRAPHY

Thelma Tate
Mabel Smith Douglass College Library
Rutgers University
Douglass Campus
New Brunswick, New Jersey

Julia Gelfand
Irvine Library
University of California at Irvine
Irvine, California

Authors

GENERAL SECTION

Mary Loe
Penfield Library
State University College of New York
Oswego, New York

Betsy Elkins
Moon Library
SUNY College of Environmental Science
    and Forestry
Syracuse, New York

ACADEMIC SECTION

Sandy Ready
Memorial Library
Mankato State University
Mankato, Minnesota

ACADEMIC SECTION (*continued*)

Sharon Stewart
McClure Education Library
University of Alabama
University, Alabama

Marvin Wiggins
Brigham Young University
Provo, Utah

COMMUNITY COLLEGE

Kathy Jordan
Northern Virginia Community College
Alexandria, Virginia

Cathy Sabol
Manassas Campus
Northern Virginia Community College
Manassas, Virginia

PUBLIC LIBRARY SECTION

Kathleen Woods
Municipal Information Library
Minneapolis, Minnesota

Helen T. Burns
Elsie Quirk Public Library
Englewood, Florida

Marilyn Barr
Ritner's Children's Branch
Free Library of Philadelphia
Philadelphia, Pennsylvania

Elizabeth J. Dailey
Onondaga County Public Library
Syracuse, New York

SCHOOL LIBRARY SECTION

Dianne Langlois
Andrew Mellon Library
Choate Rosemary Hall
Wallingford, Connecticut

Fran Corcoran
School District #62
Des Plaines, Illinois

SPECIAL LIBRARY SECTION

Tobeylynn Birch, Director
California School of Professional Psychology
Los Angeles, California

Emily Bergman
California School of Professional Psychology
Los Angeles, California

Susan J. Arrington
Government Reference Service
State Library Resource Center
Enoch Pratt Free Library
Baltimore, Maryland

PARTICIPANT SELECTION COMMITTEE

Chairperson:
J. Randolph Call
Manager, Online Systems Products and
    Services Department
OCLC
Dublin, Ohio

Marilyn Segal
Dallas, Texas

Louise Greenfield
University of Arizona
Tucson, Arizona

Lorrie Logsdon
Parlin-Ingersoll Library
Canton, Illinois

PRE-CONFERENCE WORKSHOP COMMITTEE

Chairperson:
John Tyson, University Librarian
University of Richmond
Richmond, Virginia

Dennis Clark Hamilton, Associate Librarian
Catalogue Department
University of California-Santa Barbara
Santa Barbara, California

Peggy Steele
Northwestern University Libraries
Evanston, Illinois

Jitka Hurych, Head
Department of Science and Engineering
Northern Illinois University Library
DeKalb, Illinois

Debra Park
Lincoln Trails Library System
Champaign, Illinois

EDITOR

Mary Loe, Coordinator of Library
    Instruction
State University College of New York
Oswego, New York

HANDBOOK PUBLICATION TASK FORCE

J. Randolph Call, Chairperson
Manager, Online Systems Products and
    Services Department
OCLC
Dublin, Ohio

Marilyn Barr, Children's Librarian
Ritner Children's Library
Free Library of Philadelphia
Philadelphia, Pennsylvania

May Brottman, Media Specialist
Glenbrook North High School
Northbrook, Illinois

Louise Greenfield, Instruction Librarian
University Library
University of Arizona
Tucson, Arizona

Marilyn Segal
Dallas, Texas

Index

1643